Groomed to be a Bride

Also by Maggie Hartley

Groomed to be a Bride

CAN A LOVING FOSTER CARER PROTECT
A VULNERABLE YOUNG GIRL FROM THE
NIGHTMARES OF HER PAST?

MAGGIE HARTLEY

SEVEN DIALS

First published in 2020 by Seven Dials,
an imprint of The Orion Publishing Group Ltd
Carmelite House, 50 Victoria Embankment,
London EC4Y 0DZ

An Hachette UK company

1 3 5 7 9 10 8 6 4 2

ISBN (Paperback): 978 1 409 19743 0
ISBN (eBook): 978 1 409 19744 7

Typeset by Born Group
Printed and bound in Great Britain by Clays Ltd, Elcograf S.p.A.

www.orionbooks.co.uk

Dedication

This book is dedicated to Halima, Natalie and all the children and teenagers who have passed through my home. It's been a privilege to have cared for you and to be able to share your stories. And to the children who live with me now. Thank you for your determination, strength and joy and for sharing your lives with me.

Contents

A Message from Maggie

I wanted to write this book to give people an honest account of what it's like to be a foster carer. To talk about some of the challenges that I face on a day-to-day basis and some of the children that I've helped.

My main concern throughout all this is to protect the children who have been in my care. For this reason all names and identifying details have been changed, including my own, and no locations have been included. But I can assure you that all my stories are based on real-life cases told from my own experiences.

Being a foster carer is a privilege and I couldn't imagine doing anything else. My house is never quiet but I wouldn't have it any other way. I hope perhaps my stories will inspire other people to consider fostering as new carers are always desperately needed.

Maggie Hartley

ONE

Into the Unknown

I couldn't help but smile as I opened the front door to find Louisa standing on the doorstep, but my delight soon turned to worry at the sight of Louisa's ashen face.

'Are you OK, lovey?' I asked, concerned. 'Has something happened to Charlie?'

'No, no,' she muttered vaguely. 'Charlie's fine. I just wanted to talk to you about something. Can I come in for a chat? Are you busy?'

'Of course you can, flower.' I smiled, ushering her into the hallway. 'I was just catching up with some paperwork but that can wait.'

Louisa first came into my life as a foster child when she was thirteen, after both her parents had been tragically killed in a car crash. She'd lived with me up until three years ago when she'd married her boyfriend Charlie. To all intents and purposes, she felt like my own daughter and I loved the fact that their flat was only ten minutes away. Louisa worked as a nanny for a local family and I knew today was her day off.

'You look like you could do with a cuppa,' I said to her as she followed me into the kitchen.

'Yeah, that would be good,' she said, grinning weakly.

She looked as if she'd got the weight of the world on her shoulders, but I decided to hold off on the questions until we both had a steaming mug of tea in our hands.

'So,' I said when I finally sat down at the table beside her. 'What's going on? And don't say nothing, because I can tell there's something.'

She looked away but I could see that her eyes were filled with tears.

'Louisa, lovey, you know you can tell me anything,' I urged, starting to get really worried now.

She hesitated, then took a deep breath.

'I got a bit of a shock this morning.' She paused. 'Maggie, I think I'm pregnant. I did two tests and they were both positive. I keep thinking it must be a mistake, but they're not normally wrong, are they?'

'What?' I gasped, my mind struggling to take in what she was telling me. 'But–but that's wonderful news, isn't it?'

To my surprise, Louisa just looked like she was about to burst into tears.

'I don't know,' she sighed. 'I haven't even told Charlie yet. Maggie, I don't think he's going to be happy. We want children, but we always said it was something for a few years down the line when we had more money. The flat's tiny and what on earth am I going to do about work?'

'You'll manage,' I reassured her. 'I can help out with child-care and I'm sure Charlie's parents will too. Nannies can often bring their own child to work with them, too.'

Louisa exhaled, but I was relieved to see that she was looking a little calmer now.

'I *am* pleased – it's come as a bit of a shock that's all,' she sighed. 'I've been feeling rubbish for a few weeks, but stupidly, I didn't even think. Maybe we just need some time to get our heads around the idea.'

I nodded.

'Of course you do.' I smiled, squeezing her hand. 'It's a big life change.'

I could see that just telling someone else had made Louisa feel better, and I couldn't help the rush of excitement at the thought of a new baby.

'I'd love a little boy, Maggie.' She smiled as she sipped her tea. 'Can you imagine a mini version of Charlie in some denim dungarees?'

'I can.' I grinned. 'I bet he or she is going to be very cute.'

We chatted a bit more and by the time she got up to leave, Louisa seemed a lot calmer.

'Now you look after yourself,' I told her. 'Make sure that you're eating properly and start taking folic acid straight away.'

'Yes, Mum,' she joked, rolling her eyes. 'Or should I say Granny?'

'Hey, I'm way too young to be someone's granny,' I laughed. 'I think I'll be a nan or a nanna.'

I gave her a big hug at the door.

'I'm so happy for you, flower.' I smiled. 'And I'm sure Charlie will be too when you tell him.'

'I really hope so,' she said nervously. 'I'm going to meet him after work and break it to him then.'

As I watched her walk down the path to her car, my heart was bursting with excitement for her.

Louisa was going to have a baby.

I loved everything about babies – the cuddles, their sweet smell, their tiny little clothes. I didn't even mind changing nappies. I was bursting to tell my friends Vicky and Carol but I knew I couldn't. It was early days and it wasn't my news to share. But as I cleared away the mugs, I couldn't wipe the smile off my face.

The sound of my phone ringing in my handbag on the back of the chair brought me back to the present.

'Hi, Becky,' I said as I saw the name of my supervising social worker pop up on the screen. 'How are you?'

'You sound very chirpy, Maggie,' she laughed.

'Oh, I've just had some good news,' I told her lightly. 'What can I do for you?'

'I'm actually ringing about a placement,' she replied.

And just like that, all thoughts of babies were forgotten and it was back to reality. I got a notebook and pen out of the kitchen drawer so I could write down some details if I needed to.

'Go on then,' I said, pen poised. 'Tell me more.'

Becky explained that she'd just had a call from a social worker in another county.

'She's desperately trying to find an emergency placement for a young girl who was found trying to get into the back of a lorry at a service station earlier today,' she explained. 'They think she's a refugee because she doesn't speak any English. They're currently trying to find out where she's come from and where her family are.'

'Gosh,' I gasped. 'Poor kid. She must be terrified.'

'By all accounts she is,' sighed Becky. 'She was completely on her own, she had no shoes on and hardly any belongings with her. They suspect that she's been sleeping rough for a while.'

'How old is she?' I asked.

'They don't know exactly but at a guess they think thirteen or fourteen.'

It was a lot to take in.

'So what do you think, Maggie?' asked Becky. 'Are you willing to take her on as an emergency placement? They've been contacting carers in their county but no one has the space to take her today.'

'Yes,' I said, without hesitation. 'Of course I'll take her.'

My conscience wouldn't let me turn away a frightened young girl. I couldn't even begin to imagine what she must feel like being alone in a foreign country where no one spoke her language.

'Thanks, Maggie,' sighed Becky. 'The social worker dealing with it is a woman called Penny and I know she's going to be so grateful.'

The girl was currently having a medical to assess if she was well enough to go into foster care.

'I'll phone Penny back now but I'm not sure what time they'll arrive with you,' she told me. 'Obviously she's coming from out of the area so it's probably going to be at least an hour's drive. Are you OK to wait in for the rest of the day?'

'Yes, that's fine,' I told her. 'Nat's at drama after school today and one of her friend's mums is dropping her back here, so that won't be a problem.'

Natalie was the eleven-year-old girl who had been with me for the past two months. She'd been raised by her grandmother, Peggy, as her mum, Donna, had left when she was a baby. Donna was an alcoholic and she had gone out one day and never come home. She'd got in touch from time to time over the years, but Natalie didn't have a proper relationship with her. Peggy was her world but unfortunately, earlier this year, she was diagnosed with motor neurone disease at the age of sixty-five. She was doing OK so far but there would come a point where she couldn't walk or talk and would need full-time carers, which meant that Natalie had had to come into care. She was devastated at being separated from her beloved gran, but she went round to see her three times a week and had settled in well with me.

Natalie was currently my only placement. I had a second spare bedroom that I used for fostering so I had room for another child.

'Thanks so much, Maggie,' said Becky. 'I'll pass your number on to Penny so she can let you know if there are any problems.'

'Before you go, do you know this girl's name?' I asked her.

'I'm afraid no one knows that at this point,' sighed Becky. 'Either she doesn't understand what they're asking her or she doesn't want to say. But hopefully Penny will know more by the time she gets to you.'

'OK,' I said.

As I put the phone down, I was filled with trepidation. Sometimes I didn't have much information before a child came to me, but normally at least I knew their first name and how old they were. In this case, I had absolutely nothing but a head full of questions.

Compared to when I had started fostering many years ago, there were increasing numbers of child refugees coming into the care system who had sadly arrived in the country as unaccompanied minors. So many, in fact, that some carers were now being taken on specifically to be trained to care for them. I'd fostered a couple of refugees in the past but they had both been male. Social Services had taken them in as they'd said they were teenagers. However, it had become increasingly obvious to me and their social workers that they were young men who were too old to be in the care system and were using it as a way to get accommodation. Social Services needed to be sure before they transferred them to the council.

While I waited for the new arrival, I tried to get as much ready as I could. Natalie was in the smaller single bedroom so the new girl could have the larger room, which had bunk beds and a single bed in it. The beds already had clean bedding on them as I liked to be prepared; after countless years fostering, I knew children could arrive without any warning. Even though the room was painted very neutrally, as I looked around it, I realised it was still a bit babyish for a teenage girl. The last children I'd had sleeping in there had been a three-year-old and a five-year-old who had stayed with me for three weeks while their mother was in hospital, so I moved the basket of toys, the pile of picture books and the dolls' house and put them back into the loft. Then I added a few things to try and make it feel like a more grown-up space. I put an old CD player and radio in there, as well as a pretty purple throw on the single bed and some matching cushions. I also got a navy striped rug out of the wardrobe and lay that on the floor next to the bed.

'There,' I said aloud to myself. 'That looks a lot better.'

Even just those little bits had helped to make it look more teenager than toddler. My next job was to try and dig out some clothes from my cupboards. I often picked up clothes in a few different sizes when I saw stuff on sale. When a child arrived to stay with me, I tended to take them shopping so they could choose their own things as Social Services provided them with a basic clothing allowance. But I always had spare pyjamas and underwear, and I dug out a pair of leggings and a T-shirt that were age thirteen. I also got out some clean towels, a new toothbrush and a selection of toiletries and put them on the chest of drawers in the spare room. Everything was as ready as it could be. All that was left to do now was sit and wait.

I thought I was in for a long afternoon but just after 3 p.m. there was a loud rapping on the front door. I jumped up and ran to answer it to find a tall, broad woman, who looked to be in her fifties, standing on the doorstep. She was clad in a flowing black blouse and black trousers, with a bright statement necklace and voluminous grey hair.

'You must be Maggie.' She smiled, offering me her hand and shaking mine so enthusiastically that I felt like my bones were going to break. 'I'm Penny, the social worker. Thank you so, so much for agreeing to take her on at such short notice.

'Here she is,' she said, stepping to one side to reveal a small figure cowering behind her. The girl looked back at me with huge dark frightened eyes. She was hunched over with her arms folded protectively across her chest.

'This is Halima,' she told me. 'At least, we think that's her name. Come on, pet,' she told her loudly. 'Let's go in and Maggie will show you round.'

'Come in, sweetie,' I said gently.

The girl was incredibly thin and frail with straggly long dark hair, and she was wearing a bizarre mish-mash of clothes that were way too big for her. A 'Race for Life' T-shirt, grey tracksuit bottoms that were so huge round the waist they looked like they were about to fall down any moment and a pair of flat, ballet-style black pumps that again were several sizes too big so she had to shuffle along.

'Poor love – her clothes were filthy and damp, so we cobbled together a few things that we had at the office,' explained Penny, who had obviously noticed my curious glance at what Halima was wearing.

Halima didn't seem to understand what we were saying so I held out my hand to her and beckoned her inside. She took it and as I led her into the hallway, I could feel her whole body shaking. She was absolutely petrified.

Normally when a new child arrived, especially an older one, I would take them into the living room and settle them down in front of the TV so I could talk in confidence to the social worker. But in this case, Halima probably didn't understand what we were saying, and she was so scared and bewildered that I didn't want to leave her on her own in another room.

I took her and Penny through to the kitchen where I signalled for her to sit down on the sofa. Penny sat down next to her and Halima curled up in a ball.

I filled up a glass of water and took it over to her.

'Would you like a drink?' I asked, offering the glass to her.

She looked up at me with frightened eyes and quickly shook her head.

'She's hardly said a word,' sighed Penny. 'Poor, poor love. God knows what terrible life she's escaped from. She was in such a state when she was found. No shoes, dirty clothes. We think she's been sleeping rough for a few days – thank God it's summer and it's been warm at night.

'It's OK, sweetheart,' she said to Halima loudly. 'Maggie's going to look after you now. You'll be safe here.'

Halima looked terrified as her dark eyes scanned the room.

'Do you have any idea at all about where she might have come from or where her family are?' I asked.

Penny shrugged.

'At first she wouldn't say a thing to us,' she told me. 'We got a world map out and pointed to some countries but she didn't respond. Then when we took her for the medical, one of the receptionists said Halima looked like she might be from a Middle Eastern country, so she spoke to her in Arabic and there was a definite flicker of recognition on Halima's face.

'The woman asked her in Arabic what her name was and where she had come from. All she would say was that her name was Halima, she was fifteen and she was originally from Iraq. She refused to say anything else.'

'Well at least that's something.' I smiled.

I was no political expert, but the unrest in Iraq and Syria had been on the news in the UK for many months and I couldn't begin to imagine what life must have been like there.

'I'm currently trying to sort out an Arabic translator,' added Penny. 'I'm hoping that will be sorted by tomorrow and she can come round here and try and talk to her again.'

'That would be great.' I nodded.

It would also be a chance for me to learn a few basic words in Arabic to help us communicate.

'How did her medical go?' I asked.

'Well as you can see, she's very frightened and traumatised,' sighed Penny. 'It was a female doctor but Halima refused to let her anywhere near her. The doctor said it's very likely she's underweight as she's small for her age and doesn't look well nourished. When she's a bit more settled then perhaps we can look at organising another medical, and hopefully she will feel more comfortable by then.'

'And what about school?' I asked. 'Do you want me to contact the local secondary or shall I hold off for a while?'

'I'm happy for you to get the ball rolling, but yes, I think let's get the poor child settled in a bit first before we send her off to school.'

I nodded in agreement. It was a big enough change settling in any foster child into a new school in a new area, but Halima was from a completely different country and she didn't speak the same language as her teachers and peers.

'Let's get today out of the way and get Halima settled, then I'll come back tomorrow and see how it's all going,' added Penny.

I nodded.

'Has she got anything with her?' I asked.

'Just that bag, but she won't let anyone look inside it,' said Penny. 'It's too small to have anything much in it.'

I'd noticed that when Halima came in, she was clutching a small, dirty-looking pink nylon rucksack.

'Well I can sort her out with a few things, and we can pick some other stuff up tomorrow.' I smiled.

'Maggie, I'm afraid I'm going to need to get back to the office as I've got to do a report for the police and sort out a few more things,' she told me. 'But I'll leave you my number so please do give me a call if there's anything that I can help with. I'll be in touch tomorrow and I'll come round and see Halima then.'

She stood up and gave Halima a wave.

'Bye, sweetheart. I'm going now but I will be back tomorrow, OK?'

Halima looked back at her blankly.

I walked Penny to the front door.

'Good luck, Maggie.' She smiled. 'I know it's hard when you don't speak the same language.'

'We'll get by,' I told her. 'There's a lot to be said for sign language and pointing.'

I didn't have any choice really, I just had to get on with it. But as I closed the door to Penny, I was filled with apprehension. This poor frightened girl needed comforting but we had no way of communicating. To be honest, I didn't have a clue where to start.

TWO

Signs and Signals

As I closed the front door to Penny, I took a deep breath before walking back into the kitchen.

I felt so helpless. I wanted to do all of the things that I usually did when a child first arrived, scared and bewildered. But how could I comfort her, reassure her that she was safe and make her feel welcome when we didn't even speak the same language?

Halima was still curled up in a ball on the sofa clutching her little pink bag to her chest.

'Come on, flower,' I said gently, holding out my hand to her. 'I'll give you a guided tour.'

It felt important to carry on talking to her because, for all I knew, she might understand a little bit of English, and hopefully she could pick up on my tone of voice and facial expressions. The rest of the time we'd have to get by as best we could by pointing and gesturing.

Halima stared up at me, her brown, almost black, eyes ringed with dark circles. The poor thing looked like she hadn't slept in days.

I signalled for her to come with me and, although she looked very unsure and hesitant, eventually she got up.

I took her into the living room and pointed at the TV and showed her how to turn it on with the remote.

'I'll show you your room now,' I continued.

She looked around nervously as she followed me up the stairs.

'That's my room,' I said, pointing to me and then to my bedroom.

Then I took her into her bedroom.

'And this is where you'll be sleeping,' I told her.

She looked at me blankly so I pointed at her then mimed someone asleep and made a snoring noise. I must have looked so comical, and I felt like I was acting out a nursery rhyme with a toddler. She glanced around the room at all the beds and looked even more confused.

'This one is for you,' I told her, patting the single bed. 'This is Halima's bed. OK?'

She gave me a little nod that told me she'd understood.

There was a wardrobe and a chest of drawers in the room, but I knew Halima had nothing to unpack.

I pointed to her pink bag and opened and closed the drawers.

'Put away?' I asked but she clutched the bag to her chest.

I showed her the pile of towels, the toothbrush and the toiletries that I'd put on the chest of drawers. Then I took her into the bathroom.

'Would you like a shower?' I asked her, pointing to it and then pretended to wash my hair.

Halima nodded eagerly.

So I showed her how to turn it on, then I went to get the T-shirt and leggings that I'd dug out for her as well as some clean underwear. I didn't have any bras but I did have a cropped vest top that would do for now. I put them on the side in the bathroom.

'I'll be in the kitchen if you need me,' I told her, gesturing downstairs. 'So if you need help, shout "Maggie" and I will come.'

I used two fingers to make the motion of someone walking.

She looked completely bewildered and I didn't have a clue if she understood anything that I was telling her.

I went downstairs but I didn't put the radio on and I left the kitchen door open so I could keep one ear out for Halima.

God only knows what the poor girl was thinking. I had no idea how she'd got to this country, where she'd been and what she'd left behind.

'One step at a time, Maggie,' I said aloud.

Somehow we'd just have to muddle through.

I glanced at the clock. It was after 4.30 p.m. and Natalie would be back from school soon. For dinner I'd got some bolognaise sauce out of the freezer and was going to serve it with some garlic bread and spaghetti, but I didn't have a clue if Halima would like it. Did they eat pasta in Iraq? I knew nothing about her country and I felt totally ignorant. I decided to wait until she'd had her shower and then I could show her the packet and gauge her reaction.

In the meantime, I looked at the card Penny had left me. On the back she'd written the name and number of a translator. I knew the ultimate aim was to get Halima to speak English, but in the meantime it would help me to know a few words of Arabic.

A few minutes later I heard a key in the front door and Natalie came bounding into the kitchen, her blonde ponytail swinging.

'Maggie, we're doing *Grease* for our end-of-term production and I'm gonna audition for one of the main parts,' she said excitedly as she threw her bag down on one of the chairs. 'I've brought the script back with me.'

'That's great, lovey,' I replied. 'Now before you go and get changed something happened today that I need to talk to you about . . .'

My voice trailed off as a figure suddenly appeared in the doorway. Halima stood there in a T-shirt and leggings, her long hair wet on her shoulders. She looked at Natalie with wide, terrified eyes and cowered in fear.

'Who are you?' Natalie frowned.

'Nat, this is Halima,' I told her. 'She's come to live with us for a while and she arrived this afternoon.'

Natalie looked horrified.

'But why didn't you tell me someone else was coming?'

'Lovey, I didn't know myself,' I replied. 'I only got the call from my fostering agency a few hours ago.'

Halima was frozen to the spot and was still cowering in the doorway.

'Why's she staring at me like that?' asked Natalie. 'It's so weird.'

'Halima's from Iraq and she doesn't speak any English,' I explained. 'As far as we know, she's on her own over here so she's going to stay with us until we can find out more about where she's come from and where her family are.'

'That's awful,' Natalie sighed. 'Poor thing . . . I never met no one from Iraq before,' she added, her eyes wide with curiosity. 'I don't even know where it is.'

'It's in the Middle East,' I told her.

Natalie looked confused.

'But why's she come here then if she doesn't speak English and she doesn't have anywhere to live?'

'That we don't know yet,' I said gently. 'People leave their countries for all sorts of reasons. In time, hopefully Halima will be able to tell us.'

I hated talking about Halima in front of her like this. I walked over to her.

'Halima, this is Natalie,' I said gently, pointing to her.

'Hi.' Natalie smiled shyly, giving her a little wave.

Halima looked at the floor and wouldn't make eye contact with her.

'What's wrong with her?' asked Natalie.

'I think she's just really scared, Nat,' I told her gently. 'She's in a strange country in a strange house with people she's never met before.'

'I feel really sorry for her,' she replied.

While Natalie went upstairs to get changed, I offered Halima a drink of water and she gulped it down.

'You must be hungry,' I said, rubbing my stomach. 'I'm just making dinner. Do you like pasta?' I asked, holding up the packet and showing it to her.

She shrugged.

'Well let's give it a try.' I smiled.

Fifteen minutes later, the three of us sat around the table. I looked anxiously at Halima.

'I hope you like it,' I told her.

She didn't say anything but she took a cautious mouthful, followed by another and another. Soon she was head down over her plate, spooning forkfuls of pasta into her mouth. She gulped it down hungrily and I could tell she was starving.

'I think she likes it.' Natalie smiled. 'Maybe they do have pasta in the Middle East.'

It was hard to know what to do for the rest of the evening. It felt rude to talk in front of Halima when she had no hope of joining in the conversation, or putting the TV on when she didn't understand any of it, but all we could do was carry on as normal.

'Can I watch *EastEnders*?' asked Natalie, so I put the TV on for her.

Halfway through the programme, Halima got up and walked out.

'Do you think she's OK?' asked Natalie.

'I honestly don't know.' I shrugged.

Five minutes later I went upstairs to check on her. I knocked on the bedroom door. There was no sound so I opened it to find her lying on the bed, curled up in a ball.

'Halima, are you OK?' I asked her.

She didn't answer. It was almost like she was in a trance, staring at the wall. Today's events must have all been too much for her.

'You must be so tired,' I soothed. 'Why don't you try and get some sleep?'

She looked at me with the same confused expression on her face.

This was so hard and exasperating.

I passed her the pyjamas I'd got out for her and mimed sleep. She shrugged.

'Goodnight,' I said. 'Things will seem better in the morning.'

I couldn't even begin to imagine how she must be feeling being in a country and a culture that were completely alien to her. But no matter how much I tried to reassure her, I knew it was useless because she didn't understand me.

I went back downstairs with a heavy heart.

'Is Halima OK?' asked Natalie.

'I don't really know,' I sighed. 'She's very frightened. I hope she manages to get some sleep as she seems shattered.'

Soon it was time for Natalie to go to bed too. I knew there was no way I was going to bed until I knew Halima was settled. I never slept well on a child's first night with me anyway, as I was always worrying about them and wondering how they were.

I went into the kitchen to make myself a hot chocolate. I was warming some milk on the hob when my phone beeped. It was Louisa.

I told Charlie about the baby. He was shocked but he's really happy. Excited now xx

I smiled to myself. I was so pleased for her. Our chat this morning already seemed like a lifetime ago.

I'm so happy for you both xx I wrote.

I turned off the TV and sat in the living room and had my drink. It was nice to have a few minutes of quiet just so I could sit and think. But as I sat there, I could hear someone padding about in the room above me.

It was Halima's bedroom and she was obviously not asleep yet.

I decided to give her a bit more time to settle. Half an hour later when I went up to bed, I went to check on her. I noticed the light was still on in her room, so I knocked gently on the door.

19

When I pushed it open, she was sitting up in bed, wide awake.

'Are you OK?' I asked her.

She shrugged.

'I'm going to bed now,' I told her. 'Try to get some sleep.'

I did my sleep mime again and went to turn her bedside light off. But as my hand reached over, she grabbed it and shook her head.

'Oh, OK, you don't want to be in the dark, I understand,' I told her.

'Goodnight,' I said.

I used the bathroom and went back to my bedroom but as I lay there, it was no good. I couldn't sleep.

Halima obviously wasn't asleep either. An hour later I heard her padding down the landing and the bathroom light went on.

By midnight all was quiet and I was hopeful that she had finally nodded off. But as I lay there in the darkness, I heard her get up and go to the bathroom again.

Even then she didn't settle. When she went back to her room, I could hear the floorboards creaking as she padded around. Just after 1 a.m., I saw the landing light flick on and I heard her go down the stairs.

I pulled on my dressing gown and went into to the kitchen where Halima was getting a drink of water. She jumped when she saw me.

'I'm sorry,' I soothed. 'I was just checking if you were OK?'

I put my hand on her shoulder, but she flinched.

'Do you want something to eat?' I asked her, opening up the fridge and pointing to the food inside. She quickly shook her head and scampered back up the stairs. I was at a loss. I didn't know what to do to help her settle.

I didn't sleep a wink that night and neither did Halima. She was still padding around her bedroom in the middle of the night. I was still lying there, wide awake, when it started to get light outside. Half an hour later I heard Natalie's alarm go off. Finally, I admitted defeat. I got up too and went downstairs to make a cup of tea.

As I went past Halima's bedroom, I gently knocked on the door. When I pushed it open, I could see that she was finally asleep. She was curled up on the bed in the foetal position, her dark hair spread over the pillow. I could see there was something on the floor next to her that looked as if it had dropped out of her hand. I went over and picked it up. It was a faded photo of a young couple and two children – a girl of about four or five and a boy aged about ten. They all looked so happy as they squinted in the sun.

I could tell from her face that the little girl was Halima. Was this her family in Iraq, and if so, where on earth were they now?

THREE

Speaking the Same Language

Pulling on my dressing gown, I crept downstairs as quietly as I could. Natalie was already up and dressed and making herself some breakfast in the kitchen.

'Where's Halima?' she asked as she poured herself a bowl of cornflakes.

'She's still in bed,' I told her. 'She was very unsettled last night so I'm going to let her have a little bit more sleep.'

I wished that I could have done the same. My eyes stung with tiredness and my head was spinning, but I had to get up and carry on with the day.

I made us both a cup of tea and sat at the table with Natalie while she ate her cereal.

'Why do you think she came to England?' she asked between mouthfuls. 'Where do you think her family is? Do you think she's run away?'

'I honestly don't know.' I shrugged, taking a sip of tea. 'People might leave their countries if there's a war on, if they're very poor or if they're being ill-treated and they need to make a better life for themselves. It's not something that you do lightly.'

At the moment Halima couldn't tell us what had happened to her even if she wanted to because we didn't speak her language.

'I feel really sorry for her,' sighed Natalie.

'So do I,' I replied. 'All we can hope is that she feels safe here and she feels able to tell us in her own time.'

I glanced at the clock.

'Right, lovey, you'd better get yourself off to school,' I said.

'I'm going,' she sighed. 'Remember I'm off to Nan's tonight.'

'OK. I'll check with her carer and I'll text you if there's a problem.'

Natalie went to visit Peggy three times a week after school. Her carer had my number in case Peggy wasn't well enough and was sleeping, so I could call Natalie and let her know. Lately Peggy had deteriorated very quickly and I knew it upset Natalie to see her so helpless in a wheelchair. I'd accompanied Natalie a couple of times when she had first come to live with me and Peggy was a lovely lady.

'Have a good day and I'll see you later for dinner,' I told her. 'Oh, and try not to slam the front door on your way out.'

I was keen not to disturb Halima.

'I won't,' she said, rolling her eyes.

When Natalie had gone, I was making myself a piece of toast when my phone rang. It was Penny, Halima's social worker.

'I'm just ringing to see how things are going,' she said. 'How's Halima doing?'

'She's still in bed,' I replied.

I explained how she'd had a disturbed night and had been awake for most of it.

'Oh, the poor love,' sighed Penny. 'She's obviously so traumatised by everything that she's been through. I'll pop round later to see her and don't forget to call the translator,' she added.

'I won't,' I told her. 'It's at the top of my list but I can't really do that until Halima wakes up.'

After I put the phone down to Penny, I started tidying up the breakfast things. I was carrying my dishes over to the sink when the most horrendous noise stopped me in my tracks.

A loud, piercing scream echoed through the house. It was the kind of scream that told you instantly that something was terribly wrong.

It was coming from upstairs.

My blood ran cold. The plate and mug in my hands fell to the floor and smashed to smithereens.

Ignoring the mess, I ran out into the hallway to be greeted with more screaming.

'Halima,' I yelled. 'It's OK. I'm coming.'

My heart was racing as I bolted up the stairs. I pushed open her bedroom door, terrified of what I was going to find.

But I was puzzled to find Halima lying in bed. She was screaming and crying hysterically but somehow it seemed like she was still asleep.

'Baba, Baba!' she yelled. 'La!'

Her hair was wet with sweat, and tears were streaming down her face.

'Halima,' I said loudly, gently shaking her awake. 'Halima, it's OK.'

As I shook her, I could feel her body trembling. Eventually she started to come round and she sat up, looking dazed and disorientated.

When she saw me, her eyes widened with fear and confusion.

'Halima, you're OK,' I told her gently. 'It's Maggie, remember? You're staying at my house.'

She blinked, her eyes wet with tears. She looked utterly terrified and she was struggling to breathe.

'You're OK,' I repeated, putting my hand on her shoulder. 'You were having a bad dream.'

I knew she couldn't understand what I was saying but I was hoping that the tone of my voice would help to calm and reassure her. Again, I felt utter frustration that neither of us could understand each other.

'Would you like a drink?' I asked her, pointing to the empty glass on her bedside table.

She nodded, not making eye contact with me.

By the time I'd filled up the glass in the bathroom and come back, she had composed herself. Her face was still pale and she looked exhausted but she seemed calmer now.

'Would you like to come and get some breakfast?' I asked.

I passed her a dressing gown and mimed eating. Then I gestured that I was going downstairs to give her a little bit of time to use the bathroom and fully wake up.

As I swept the broken crockery off the kitchen floor, I didn't know what to think. I felt so helpless. Halima had been extremely distressed but I didn't know who or what she was shouting about and there was nothing really that I could do to reassure her.

Ten minutes later she came downstairs. She'd got dressed in the clothes that I'd got out for her yesterday. She was still very timid and she didn't make eye contact with me as she sat down at the table. I put some cereal boxes in front of her and some slices of bread and jam and butter but she shook her head. The only thing she managed was a cup of black tea and an orange that she took out of the fruit bowl.

While she was eating, I got the card out that Penny had left with the translator's details on the back. His name was Amir and he was approved by the local authority to work as a translator for children in care. He could be based anywhere in the country, but he was specially trained in safeguarding issues, so he knew to raise them if a child said anything to him. I just desperately wanted someone to talk to Halima for me and check that she was OK.

I called the number and when he picked up the phone, I explained who I was.

'Ah yes, I spoke to Penny yesterday and she said you'd be in touch,' he told me.

He was friendly and he had a warm manner.

'Is Halima with you now?' he asked. 'What is it that you'd like me to ask or tell her?'

I had so many burning questions that I wanted to know the answers to, but I knew this wasn't the time or the place. My main aim today was to make Halima feel relaxed and comfortable. I didn't want to upset her or put pressure on her by getting a stranger on the phone to ask her potentially upsetting and traumatic questions about her journey here or her life back in Iraq. Those sorts of questions could come in time and they needed to be asked when Penny was here.

'I just want to check that she's OK really,' I told him. 'Could you explain to her that for the time being, she's going to be staying here with me and Natalie, and that her social worker Penny is going to come round and see her later on today.'

'OK,' he said.

'Could you also tell her that I'm going to take her shopping this morning to choose some clothes and is there anything in particular that she needs?'

'That's fine,' he told me. 'Do you want to put Halima on now and I can introduce myself?'

While I had been talking, Halima had just been sitting staring into space. When I passed her the phone, she looked suspiciously at me.

'Listen,' I told her, pointing to my ear. 'Arabic.'

Hesitantly, she held it to her ear. As Amir began to speak, I could see a flicker of recognition in Halima's eyes.

'Marhaban,' she said in a quiet voice.

She nodded as he talked away to her on the other end of the line.

'Nem.' She nodded. 'Naam hasananaan.'

I had no idea what she was saying and a few minutes later she handed the phone back to me.

'What did she say?' I asked, intrigued.

'Not a lot,' he told me. 'I passed on the information that you had given me and she said that she was fine and that she understood. She didn't seem to want to say anything more.'

It was disappointing but I could understand why she didn't want to open up to a strange man on the end of the phone.

'Before you go, please could you teach me a few basic words in Arabic?' I asked him.

I at least wanted to be able to say hello and goodbye to Halima and ask if she was OK.

'Of course,' he said.

I knew I was probably spelling them incorrectly, but I wrote them down as they were pronounced.

'I've probably got these completely wrong but at least I can try,' I told him.

'Have faith,' he laughed. 'At least you're willing to give it a go.'

'Thank you,' I said.

'Oh, and if you've got satellite TV you can sometimes pick up Arabic TV programmes or radio shows that Halima might enjoy,' he told me.

I thanked him for the tip and put the phone down. Halima was picking on a piece of bread and jam and I was pleased to see that she was eating. I looked down at the piece of paper in my hand.

'Kayfa haluki?' I asked hesitantly.

My pronunciation must have been terrible as a tiny smile broke out on Halima's face.

'Hasananaan,' she replied.

I was trying to ask how she was and as I looked down at my scribbled notes, I realised joyfully that she had replied that she was OK.

'That's great.' I smiled, giving her a thumbs up. 'You're OK. I understand.'

She probably thought I was mad but at least we'd had a tiny bit of communication and I didn't feel quite as useless.

However, it was back to sign language as I handed her some shoes that looked like they would fit and tried to mime that we were going to the shops. Hopefully she would understand as I'd asked Amir to tell her we were going to do this. But her face was etched with worry as she followed me out to the car.

'Shops,' I told her as we pulled up at the retail park a few minutes' drive from my house.

I'd normally try to kit children out at the beginning with less expensive clothes from the supermarket so that I could get a lot more out of their clothing allowance. However, as Halima was older, I took her into Next. The store was bright and noisy and filled with people and I could see that she was on edge, so I knew I needed to try and get this over with as quickly as possible. I didn't have a clue what she liked but I pulled out a few things in her size and showed them to her. There were some T-shirts and a hoodie, some jeans and a denim jacket.

I didn't want to put her through having to try them on in a noisy hot changing room. Thankfully she gave them all a thumbs up and I then picked out a pair of trainers in a size five that seemed to fit her, plus some pyjamas and underwear.

After that we went into Asda. Halima looked amazed as we walked up and down the huge aisles of food.

'You choose,' I told her, pointing to the fruit and vegetables. Hesitantly she picked up a pomegranate and looked at me expectantly as if asking whether could she have it.

'Yes, of course.' I smiled, putting it in the trolley.

As we walked round the store, slowly she got more confident. She picked out some fresh herbs, some hummus and pitta breads and some dried spices I'd never even heard of.

'I hope you're going to show me what to do with those,' I said.

I was pleased to see that, although she still wouldn't hold eye contact with me for very long, Halima did at least seem a little bit more relaxed than she had that morning.

After we'd finished our shopping, we headed home. As I pulled into my street, I noticed there was a car parked outside my house that I didn't recognise. I guessed it must be Penny.

'I was just about to call you,' she said as she walked over to us.

'Sorry, we needed to go and get Halima some clothes and she picked some food out.'

'How are you, Halima?' Penny boomed.

She seemed to think that talking loudly would somehow help make Halima understand what she was saying. But Halima looked terrified.

I rummaged in my handbag for the piece of paper that I'd written the Arabic phrases on.

'Kayfa haluki?' I asked hesitantly.

Halima nodded and gave me a weak smile.

Penny's eyes almost popped out of her head.

'I didn't realise that you spoke Arabic, Maggie,' she said, looking stunned.

'I don't,' I said. 'But I asked the translator for a few basic words and phrases.'

When we'd got inside the house, I gave Halima the bags with her new clothes in them and she took them upstairs. Penny and I went into the kitchen and I put the kettle on.

'So what happens now?' I asked her.

'My main priority is to find a translator who can talk to Halima face to face so we can start to ask her a few more questions,' she told me. 'We need to try and work out how she got here and where her family are.'

'She didn't say much at all to the translator on the phone this morning,' I said. 'So I think face to face would work much better. I also think it's more likely that Halima will open up if it's a woman.'

I definitely thought a teenage girl would feel more relaxed and relate better to another female rather than a man.

'That's a good point,' Penny agreed. 'I also think going to school will help,' she went on. 'The best and quickest way to learn a language is to immerse yourself in it and I think Halima could perhaps do with some structure to her day.'

'Do you think it's too much, too soon?' I asked her. Halima had only just arrived, and I didn't want to overwhelm her any more than we already had.

'I think by the time we've put the wheels in motion, been to visit the school and sorted out the uniform etc, then it's going to take well over a week,' replied Penny. 'So hopefully Halima will feel more ready for it by then.'

I agreed to make contact with the local secondary school that Natalie attended. My only concern was that it was largely a very white school with little racial diversity.

'Well, let's see what they could put in place in terms of language assistance,' Penny said. 'Other than school and rescheduling her medical, there isn't a huge amount we can do at this time.'

I told Penny how Halima had been screaming and crying in her sleep.

'The poor girl has clearly been through a lot,' she sighed. 'More than anything, we desperately need to know where she's come from and where on earth her family is.'

The sooner Halima started talking to us, the better.

FOUR

Lost in Translation

Penny kept to her word. The following day she called me to let me know that she'd found a female Arabic speaker who could come over to the house. She was a support worker at Penny's office and she'd offered to help us translate.

'Her name's Fatima, she's twenty-seven and she's Syrian,' she told me. 'I thought it would be good to have someone younger as Halima might feel more at ease and be more likely to open up to her.'

'Yes, I think you're right,' I replied.

Halima had been with me for three days now and we desperately needed her to start talking to us. Every morning I'd called Amir and told him what we were doing that day and given him any other information that I needed to pass on to Halima and he'd relayed it to her in Arabic. I always asked him to check that she was OK but she just gave him one-word answers and hadn't volunteered any other information or wanted him to ask me any questions. She was still very closed and shut down.

As far as we knew, Halima was an unaccompanied minor, so she had a right to stay in this country. But Social Services were keen to know how and why she had come to the UK and where her family was, in case they could reunite them.

I also wanted to be able to offer her help or try to get counselling or therapy if she needed it. All the signs were there that Halima had been through some sort of trauma.

She was still very unsettled at night and always struggled to get to sleep. Even when she did sleep, she would scream and cry out.

It meant that every night I was on tenterhooks, listening out for her and worrying whether she was OK. I was worn out surviving on a few hours' sleep and Halima looked constantly shattered too.

There was one word that she kept yelling again and again in her sleep. I'd made a note of it and asked Amir.

'What does "baba" mean?' I'd asked him casually when Halima was out of earshot.

'It's an Arabic term for father or dad,' he'd explained.

'And "la"?' I'd asked.

'That means no.'

So she'd been shouting out 'No, Dad'. I was confused. Was she crying out because she was scared of her father and he was doing something she didn't want him to? Or was she crying because something had happened to him or he was being hurt? At this point in time there was absolutely no way of knowing.

It was a relief to know that Penny had found someone to come and help us talk to Halima face to face. At least we could try to ask those difficult questions.

'I'm hoping Fatima will be able to come over tomorrow, but I'll ring you later to confirm,' Penny told me.

I knew Natalie was finding it hard too.

'I feel like I'm being horrible because I'm not saying nothing to her but there's no point cos she doesn't understand,' she sighed.

'I know.' I nodded. 'It's difficult for everyone.'

My few basic words of Arabic only went so far, and I could see the endless sign language, gesturing and pointing was exhausting for Halima too. I was acutely aware of the fact that she must feel so alone and isolated when Natalie and I were chatting away.

Later that afternoon, Halima was watching some Arabic programmes on TV while I collected some washing from her room. I lifted back her duvet in a bid to try and find her pyjamas when I noticed something sticking out from under her pillow. It was the faded photograph that Halima had been clutching in her sleep the first night that she'd come here. I picked it up to look at it more closely just as Halima walked into the room.

'It's a lovely photo.' I smiled.

'Is that your father?' I asked, pointing to the dark-haired man in the photo who was wearing a shirt and tie. Suddenly I remembered the Arabic word.

'Baba?' I asked.

Her face fell and she snatched the photograph out of my hands, clutching it to her chest.

'Halima, I'm so sorry,' I told her. 'I just wanted to find out more about you.'

I put my hand on her shoulder but she shrugged me off.

She had tears in her eyes as she walked out of the room.

I felt like I'd totally let her down and betrayed her trust, but I was just curious to learn more about her family and where she'd come from.

As far as I was concerned, this face-to-face session couldn't come soon enough.

I was even more worried that afternoon when I was cleaning the bathroom and noticed that the small stainless steel bin was stuffed full of strips of white fabric. My heart sank when I saw that they were soaked with blood.

I noticed a label on one of the scraps and I realised that they were bits of ripped-up pillowcase. It was from old bedding that I kept in the wardrobe in Halima's bedroom.

I'd seen these signs before with other children and it filled me with absolute horror.

Was Halima self-harming?

I hadn't noticed any marks on her arms or body, but I knew that children would often cut or scratch themselves where the wounds couldn't easily be seen. I found the bin in the downstairs loo was filled with the same bloody pieces of fabric too.

I knew I needed to mention my worries to Penny.

When my phone rang, I was expecting it to be her calling me back so I was surprised to see Louisa's number on the screen.

'Hello, flower, how are you?' I asked her.

'Really sick,' she croaked. 'Every morning I've had my head down the toilet.'

'Oh, you poor thing,' I replied. 'It's all those hormones kicking in.'

'It's horrible, Maggie,' she sighed.

I could tell by the tone of her voice she felt rotten. I'd texted her when Halima had first arrived to say that I had a new placement but, even so, I suddenly felt guilty that I hadn't been in touch.

'I'm sorry I haven't rung you for a few days,' I told her. 'I've been so busy trying to get Halima settled.'

'How is she doing?' she asked.

'I don't know really,' I sighed.

I explained what had happened and that we didn't know much more than we did when she first arrived.

'The language issue is obviously a real barrier,' I said. 'But hopefully we're getting a translator to come round tomorrow so fingers crossed that Halima starts talking to us. It's probably a bit much for her to meet new people at the moment, but pop in later in the week if you feel up to it?'

'I'll see,' Louisa sighed. 'I'm just shattered by the time I get back from work.'

'You look after yourself,' I told her.

As I put the phone down, I couldn't help but smile at the thought of having a grandchild in a few months. With Halima's arrival, I still hadn't had the chance to digest Louisa's news properly.

Half an hour later Penny called back to confirm that she and Fatima would come round in the morning.

'I'll chat to her before we come and fill her in on what we know so far and what we'd like to ask her, and we'll take it from there,' she told me.

I also told her my suspicions about Halima possibly hurting herself.

'Oh no,' she sighed. 'I really hope that you're wrong, Maggie, but it's something we can get Fatima to talk to her about tomorrow.'

'I hope so too.' I nodded.

Since I'd found those rags, I hadn't wanted to take my eyes off Halima for a minute, I was so paranoid that she was hurting herself.

That night as I went to bed, I felt utter relief. Relief that tomorrow we might get some proper answers from Halima that would allow us all to move forward.

For the first time in days, I actually slept for more than a few hours and I woke up feeling a lot better. I didn't call Amir as normal because I knew Fatima would soon be here with Penny and she could explain everything to Halima. Just after 9 a.m. there was a knock on the door and I went to open it.

'Morning, Maggie,' chirped Penny, bustling in and filling the hallway with the pungent smell of hairspray.

'This is Fatima,' she said, gesturing to the pretty young woman standing next to her. She was wearing a hijab and was trendily dressed in ripped jeans and Reebok trainers.

'Hi, Fatima,' I smiled. 'Come on in.'

Halima, who had been in the kitchen, poked her head curiously around the door.

'Halima, this is Fatima,' I told her.

She stared shyly at her.

'As-salamu alaikum,' said Fatima, bowing her head.

Halima looked surprised.

'Wa alaikumus-salam wa rahmatullah,' she replied, bowing her head too.

Penny and I looked at each other quizzically.

'It's a common Muslim greeting,' explained Fatima.

It was the most that I'd heard Halima say in the past three days. I must admit, I hadn't thought about her religion or the fact that she might be Muslim.

Fatima continued speaking in Arabic to her to explain, I guessed, who she was and why she was there and Halima was silently taking it all in.

'Shall we go into the living room then?' suggested Penny.

I showed them all in and got them settled, then went into the kitchen to make everyone a drink.

When I came back in, Fatima was still chatting to Halima, who was listening intently.

I put down the tray of tea.

'I was just telling Halima about my grandparents back in Syria and how my family has been in this country since I was thirteen,' she told us.

Penny nodded.

'Perhaps this would be a good time for you to ask Halima about her family and where they are?' she suggested.

Fatima nodded and began talking to Halima in Arabic while Penny and I watched nervously. Her tone was really gentle, but Halima's face dropped and she stared at the floor.

'In 'ukhbirak,' she muttered, shaking her head.

Fatima continued talking; however, I could tell by Halima's body language that it wasn't going well. She curled up in a protective ball like she had done on the first day that she'd arrived.

'In 'ukhbirak,' she told her, more firmly this time.

Fatima turned to Penny and me and shrugged.

'I asked her about her family in Iraq but she said she's sorry but she doesn't want to talk about it,' she explained. 'I really don't want to push it too much and upset her.'

'No, no of course not,' sighed Penny. 'That's not what we want either. How about we all have a drink?' she said brightly, clearly trying to lighten the mood in the room.

I passed Halima a black tea but she shook her head and buried it in her hands.

The three of us chit-chatted for a while, but Halima stayed curled up tight.

'While Fatima is here, Maggie, is there anything that you'd like her to ask Halima?' Penny asked.

At this point in time I knew it was best to stick to something that wasn't contentious.

'I'd like her to know that we're going to try and get her settled into a school in the next few days,' I replied. 'We'll be going to visit it so it would be useful to know if she had been to school in Iraq.'

I held my breath as Fatima asked her the question. Halima looked at her with wide eyes and nodded. At least she didn't mind answering that.

'Could you also ask her if she's comfortable in my home and is there anything that she wants?' I told her. 'It would be good to know if she has any religious or cultural needs.'

I paused.

'And there's something else too. I'm not sure how you want to phrase this but it's something I really do have to ask about as it's a safeguarding issue.'

I paused and looked over at Penny and she nodded.

'Yesterday I noticed quite a lot of rags in the bin with blood on them and we're worried that Halima has been hurting herself. If she has, then I'd really like to be able to help her.'

Fatima talked to Halima and she shook her head. She replied to her in Arabic and looked very embarrassed. Fatima nodded and put her hand on Halima's.

'She said she hasn't been hurting herself. She has her period but she didn't have the right words to tell you, so she used the rags.'

I was mortified.

'Oh the poor girl,' gasped Penny. 'Maggie, can you sort her out with some pads or tampons?'

'Yes, of course,' I replied. I felt absolutely terrible that I'd thought she was self-harming, and that I hadn't thought to provide her with some pads.

We chatted for a little while longer. Halima was quiet but at least she stayed in the room and drank her tea.

'I know you've got to get back to the office, Fatima, but while you're here shall we give it one last go?' Penny asked her. 'Could you perhaps talk to Halima and see if she's willing to tell us how she got to the UK?'

'I can try.' She shrugged.

She turned to Halima and started talking. Halima started shaking her head again, babbling away in Arabic. I could tell that she was angry. She said something very angrily, burst into tears and stormed out of the room.

Fatima looked tearful too.

'She said she doesn't want to talk about how she got here and to leave her alone,' she sighed.

'Don't worry,' Penny told her. 'It's not your fault.'

'I should at least go and see how she is,' I said, about to get up.

'Can I go?' asked Fatima. 'I'd like to apologise for upsetting her.'

'And at least she can understand you,' added Penny.

While Fatima went to see Halima in the kitchen, Penny and I had a chat.

'Well, that didn't work out as well as we'd hoped,' sighed Penny. 'She really doesn't seem to want to answer any questions.'

I nodded. I realised that she hadn't told us whether she was religious or not either. I knew that Iraq was a predominantly Muslim country, but I had no idea whether Halima was actively practising or not.

'It's really frustrating but we've got to accept that it's going to take time for Halima to want to tell us,' I said. 'Perhaps I was a bit naive expecting Halima to talk about traumatic, upsetting things to people that she's only just met.'

'How is she?' asked Penny when Fatima came back in.

'She's OK,' she said. 'She understands that everyone cares about her and wants to help her. She just doesn't feel able to talk about things yet. I can see it's very painful for her.'

I understood.

'She's a sweet girl,' said Fatima. 'I'm happy to come round again or you can ring me and I can talk to her on the phone.'

'Why don't you pop round in a couple of days for a cup of tea?' I suggested. 'No asking heavy questions or passing on information, just purely a social thing. Hopefully Halima will start to feel more comfortable.'

Penny nodded.

'I'll talk about it with Fatima's line manager but that sounds like a great idea,' she said.

Just because Fatima spoke the same language as her didn't automatically mean that Halima was going to open up and tell her everything. It takes time to build up a relationship and to know that you can trust someone, and I had started to realise that we were in this for the long haul.

FIVE

Familiarity

Another day, another challenge for Halima. Today we were going to have a meeting with the head teacher at Halima's new secondary school and as we pulled up into the car park, I could see that she was nervous. Fatima and I got out of the car but she hung back and refused to get out.

'Hasananaan?' I asked her, which meant 'OK?' in Arabic. It was one of the words I had remembered and used frequently.

Halima shook her head, her brown eyes filled with tears.

'Please can you talk to her, Fatima, and see if you can reassure her?' I asked her.

'Of course,' she said.

I was so pleased and relieved that Fatima had been able to come with us today, otherwise the prospect of going to the school would have been even more daunting. The head teacher was going to show us around and at least Halima would be fully on board with what was happening if Fatima was there to explain things.

Not only Natalie but previous foster children had attended this secondary school. The head, Ms Hicks, was relatively new but I'd met her before when a girl called Hannah, whom I'd fostered recently, had gone there for a few months.

'She says she's nervous about going to school in this country and about not being able to speak the language,' Fatima explained.

I put my arm on Halima's shoulder.

'Tell her that it's OK, we're all here for her and I think she's being really brave.' I smiled. 'Also tell her that I've met the head teacher before and she's really lovely.'

I understood how Halima felt. Starting a new school was daunting for any teenager, never mind one who was in a completely new country and didn't speak the language. To be honest, I was worried too. The area wasn't ethnically diverse, and the school community reflected that and was largely white British. I was also unsure how on earth they were going to teach someone who didn't speak English.

Thankfully, Fatima seemed to reassure Halima, and it was a relief when she finally got out of the car and we all walked towards the reception. We'd arranged to come in after the school day had finished so the building would be much quieter and less intimidating for Halima.

We signed in and a few minutes later, Ms Hicks, a smartly dressed woman in her forties, came out to meet us. She was one of those head teachers who was very dynamic and had a real air of authority about them but was approachable at the same time.

'Nice to see you again, Ms Hartley,' she said in her broad Scottish accent.

'Oh, please call me Maggie,' I told her, smiling. 'This is Halima, who's going to be starting at the school, and Fatima, who's going to translate everything into Arabic for her so she understands what we're saying.'

'Ah that's great,' she replied. 'I did wonder how it was going to work.'

'Welcome,' she said to Halima, who had edged behind Fatima and still looked terrified.

Ms Hicks took us into her office and we all sat down. Halima looked shyly at the floor, avoiding eye contact, as Ms Hicks began to talk to her.

'Well, Halima, we're looking forward to you starting here,' she told her kindly. 'I know it must be really terrifying coming somewhere where no one speaks your language, but we're going to do our very best to help you learn English and I'm sure you'll pick it up in no time.'

Fatima repeated what she had said to Halima and she gave a weak smile.

'Does Halima have anything that she wants to ask me?' Ms Hicks enquired.

Fatima asked in Arabic but Halima quickly shook her head.

'Maggie, I know you've been to the school before but I've arranged for Halima to be shown round by one of our pupils,' she said. 'And, of course, Fatima can go too and help translate.'

Fatima was just repeating everything in Arabic for Halima when there was a knock on the door.

'This is Ellie and she's in year ten,' said Ms Hicks. 'She's going to give you a guided tour.'

A tall girl with braces and in school uniform smiled. As Fatima and Ellie headed for the door, Halima looked uncertain. I nodded and gave her a thumbs up.

'You go with them,' I told her, gesturing to the door. 'It's OK.'

She still looked very on edge as she followed them out.

'Poor girl,' sighed Ms Hicks. 'She seems very lost.'

'She is.' I nodded. 'As I said to you on the phone the other day, we know she's from Iraq but apart from that we have very little other information. We don't know anything about her family, why or how she came to this country and how long she's been here. I'm hoping that in time she will start to trust us enough to tell us more.'

Ms Hicks nodded.

'Is there anything you want to ask me, Maggie?' she said.

My main worry was how the school was going to cope with the language barrier.

'How on earth do you begin to teach someone who doesn't speak English?' I asked.

'Maggie, you obviously know our school,' replied Ms Hicks. 'We're not the most multicultural in terms of our students and catchment area and we don't have many pupils for whom English is a second language. But I have had experience teaching refugee children in the past, and what I've found works best is total immersion. We speak to them in English in lessons and we expect them to speak back to us in English too.

'It's tricky at the start, especially when it comes to written work, but I'm confident that within a few weeks of Halima being here, her spoken English will have dramatically improved.'

All I could hope was that she was right.

'I feel helpless as to what to do to support her. We suspect she's been through some sort of trauma, but she hasn't felt ready or able to disclose to us what's happened to her yet,' I sighed.

'Well, I think school will help,' replied Ms Hicks. 'It will be hard at first, but we'll do our very best to make sure she settles.

'And hopefully in a few weeks she will have made friends and will be coming on in leaps and bounds with her language.'

'I hope so,' I sighed. 'I just feel very frustrated not being able to help her.'

'I'm sure you are,' smiled Ms Hicks. 'But you're giving her a home, a routine and stability, and that means a lot.'

'I suppose so,' I said.

Ms Hicks also had some good news to share.

'After I'd put down the phone to you the other day, Maggie, I realised that one of our office staff, Mrs Savage, can speak some Arabic. Her mother is from Jordan, I believe, and she's kindly offered to sit with Halima in certain lessons like English, just until she finds her feet.

'She'll also be available to help with communication between Halima and her teachers just to get her through the first few weeks until she picks up more of the language.'

'That's great,' I sighed. 'I know she'll really appreciate that.'

'And, Maggie, you know you can phone me at any time if you've got any problems or you want to talk,' she added.

'Thank you,' I said gratefully. 'And Halima will have Natalie here too, so at least there will be one familiar face.'

'Oh yes, of course,' said Ms Hicks.

I left her office feeling slightly more reassured. As we walked out to reception, Halima and Fatima were just coming back from their tour.

'So how was it?' asked Ms Hicks. 'What did you make of our school, Halima?'

Fatima repeated it in Arabic and Halima nodded and said something back. I was relieved to see her smiling shyly.

'She said it's very big, but she really liked the art block.'

'Oh, you like art! That's great.' Ms Hicks smiled. 'We have a thriving art department.'

Halima looked a little less terrified as we walked back towards the car.

'All good?' I asked and she gave me a little nod.

Penny and I had talked about it and we had decided that in order to give Halima time to get used to the idea and for me to have chance to sort out a uniform, she would start school the following week. She would have been with me for almost a fortnight by then.

Every day was a case of taking little steps. I didn't want to bombard Halima all at once as everything was still so new, but I tried to sort out one thing each day. I was really grateful to have Fatima's help. She couldn't come round every day, but she was always at the end of the phone if we found ourselves really stuck.

It was a day of appointments, as Penny had also rearranged Halima's Looked After Child (LAC) medical to the afternoon following the visit to school. After Halima's initial refusal when she'd first come into care, Penny had booked us into the local medical centre. As we drove across town from the school, Fatima explained to Halima what was going to happen.

I looked in the rear-view mirror to gauge her response, and saw Halima shaking her head vigorously and saying something in Arabic.

'She said she doesn't want to do it,' Fatima sighed.

'Please tell her it's nothing to worry about,' I told her. 'It's just important for us to check that she's OK and to make sure she doesn't have any medical conditions we need to know about.'

From the name Penny had given me, I knew the doctor wasn't one that I'd met before, but as she worked with Social Services, she would be specially trained to deal with traumatised children. When we pulled up outside the medical centre, though, Halima refused to get out of the car again.

She was scowling as she something in Arabic to Fatima.

'She said she doesn't want to do it and there's nothing wrong with her,' Fatima explained.

'Please reassure her that it's a female doctor and it's nothing to worry about,' I pleaded. 'We can talk her through exactly what will happen, but the doctor will want to check her height and weight and ask her a few questions about her health.'

Fatima relayed the information to Halima.

'She said what sort of questions?' asked Fatima.

'All sorts,' I explained. 'If she's ever been in hospital or is on any medication, if there's any family history of illnesses. Nothing at all to worry about.'

But when Fatima repeated it all to Halima, she shook her head. I could see her body was trembling with fear.

'She said she's not answering any questions and she doesn't want to do it.'

49

This time she refused point-blank to get out of the car. I called Penny on my mobile and told her what was happening.

'There's nothing we can do really,' she sighed. 'We can't force her to have a medical if she isn't willing to co-operate.'

I could see that Halima's whole demeanour had changed the moment we'd mentioned her family. Anything connected to that and she just seemed to shut down.

I didn't want to cause Halima any more distress after what had already been a stressful day.

I said goodbye to Penny, and gave Halima a weak smile.

'Tell her it doesn't matter and that I didn't mean to upset her,' I told Fatima.

Halima slumped in her seat and didn't say a word.

We had a quiet rest of the day and that night my boyfriend Graham called. He was a physiotherapist in his forties and we'd been together for a few years. I'd spoken to him a couple of days after Halima had arrived, but he'd been at a conference since then.

'You know how you told me the new girl you were fostering was from Iraq?' he said. 'Well, after we'd spoken, I remembered that my friend Paul's wife Emaa is from Iraq too.'

'Oh yes,' I said. 'I remember her.'

We had gone round to their house for a barbecue a couple of years ago. I knew she was from a Middle Eastern country, but I had forgotten that it was Iraq.

'Well I bumped into Emaa at the supermarket today and I hope you don't mind, but I mentioned to her that you were fostering an Iraqi refugee and she said why don't you bring her round for dinner?'

He paused.

'I know you like to keep your fostering separate from our relationship, but I thought it might be good for this girl to be around someone else from her own country.'

'Of course, I don't mind,' I told him. 'That's a really nice idea. I'll ask Halima and see what she says.'

He gave me Emaa's number and I promised to call her.

I was sure it would be nice for Halima to be around people from her culture, but it would also be good for me too. I knew nothing about Iraq and I wanted to learn about her culture too and help her feel more settled. Everything so far had been about Halima fitting in with us, learning our language and eating our food, so it would be comforting for her to experience something familiar.

I rang Emaa straight away. She was very warm and bubbly.

'Maggie, of course I remember you,' she said. 'Graham told me about Halima and I'd love to meet her. Bring her round and I'll make us all some dinner.'

'I'd be so grateful,' I told her. 'I'm sure she'd love to spend some time with someone else from Iraq.'

A couple of nights later we went round. I'd got Fatima to explain to Halima over the phone what we were doing. She didn't seem overly enthusiastic about it, but she had come without making a fuss. She was shy and timid around new people, which was understandable, and why I'd kept things low-key. Louisa hadn't met her yet and none of my friends had been round as I was worried it would be too much for her.

Paul and Emaa lived a twenty-minute drive from my house in a row of terraces, a few doors down from Graham. He'd already said he didn't want to come in case it was too much for Halima, which, to be honest, I was relieved about.

I knocked at the door and Emaa opened it with a wriggling baby on her hip.

'Hi, Maggie,' she said with a smile. 'I'm so pleased you could come. And you must be Halima.'

'Marhaban,' Emaa said to her. 'Kayfa haluki?'

'Naam hasananaan,' she replied.

'Come in, come in,' Emaa said, ushering us into the living room where Paul was playing with their four-year-old daughter Hattie.

'This is William, my one-year-old,' she told us. 'I hadn't had him last time we met, Maggie.'

Paul and Emaa were so welcoming, and although she was quiet, Halima seemed quite relaxed. Her face lit up when she saw the children and she sat down on the floor and started to play with Hattie.

Emaa, Paul and I went out into the kitchen.

'Whatever's cooking smells delicious,' I said, savouring the spices in the air.

'Ah, I've made us some traditional Iraqi dishes,' she replied.

'I'm so grateful to you for doing this,' I told her. 'It'll be good for Halima to have something familiar and someone who can chat to her.'

'My Arabic is a bit hit and miss, but I still remember quite a lot so it's nice to have someone to practise on,' Emaa said.

I'd explained on the phone some of the difficulties I'd been having, and I was touched when she passed me an English–Arabic dictionary that she'd dusted off.

'I thought this might help a little bit with the communication,' she said to me. 'Obviously you can't read Arabic, but it has got the pronunciation in it, which should help.'

'Thank you,' I said, smiling. 'I know a few basic phrases, but this will be really useful.'

Emaa also assured me that everything that we were eating was halal.

'Oh, I'm not sure Halima is a practising Muslim,' I told her. 'If she is, she hasn't mentioned it.' Halima hadn't arrived wearing a hijab and she hadn't asked for one. It was another thing that I hoped she would talk to us about in her own time.

'Hmm, that's very unusual. Most Iraqis are Muslim.' Emaa shrugged.

I went to check on Halima. She was playing with the baby and Hattie was sitting on her knee.

'She's made a friend there,' laughed Emaa.

She went and joined them on the floor and chatted away to Halima in Arabic.

Paul and I stayed in the kitchen.

'I noticed Emaa doesn't wear a headscarf,' I said. 'Is she a Muslim?'

'She was raised Muslim but she's not practising any more,' he said. 'I know her grandparents and mother were, but sadly they're all dead now.'

Soon it was time for dinner and Emaa had made the most delicious feast. I saw Halima's face light up as she sat down at the table and saw all the dishes laid out.

Emaa talked me through what each of the dishes was. There were some cabbage leaves stuffed with rice, a lamb, okra and tomato stew, and some rice, yogurt and hummus. It was all absolutely delicious and I enjoyed every bite, but the best thing was seeing Halima's face as she savoured every mouthful.

'I can see how much she's enjoying it.' I smiled.

Afterwards Halima went to help Emaa clear up in the kitchen and I read Hattie a story while Paul got William ready for bed.

I was pleased to hear Emaa chatting away in the kitchen to Halima in Arabic and she was responding.

For the first time in days, it seemed as though she had relaxed. She wasn't curled up in a protective ball, afraid to make eye contact, or rocking back and forth.

I was very thankful to Graham for coming up with the idea. All the time we'd been together, I'd kept my fostering life separate from our relationship. It made things a lot simpler. I had chosen this life and he hadn't. There was also the added complication that him being involved would mean him having to undergo endless Social Services checks.

Soon it was late, and I realised Emaa and Paul needed to put Hattie to bed. Before we left, I went to say goodbye to Emaa who was in the kitchen making William a bottle.

'I can't thank you enough for tonight,' I told her. 'It's the first time I've seen Halima let her guard down.'

'She's a very sweet girl,' she said. 'I feel so sorry for her though. I left Iraq more than twenty years ago when I was a teenager. I can't imagine what things are like there now since the war started.'

'Did she say anything to you about her family or where she had come from?'

Emaa shook her head.

'I didn't want to upset her or ask her any questions,' she told me. 'She did say one thing though that I thought was very poetic, although it was very sad too.'

'Oh, what was that?' I asked.

'Her exact words were "I can't sleep at night because every time I close my eyes I'm haunted by the pictures that I have in my head." And when I asked her what she meant, what those pictures were, she clammed up and said she could never tell anyone.'

One day she will, I told myself. One day she will open up and tell us how and why she had come to the UK. She had to.

SIX

Memories

A few weeks later, there was a knock at the door and when I went to open it, Louisa was standing on the doorstep.

'What a lovely surprise!' I exclaimed, delighted to see her and pulling her in for a hug.

'I knew the girls would be at school, so I thought I'd pop in for a coffee,' she said.

'How are you, lovey?' I asked, as we walked through to the kitchen. 'How's the bump?'

Louisa proudly patted her stomach, which was still tiny.

'I feel massive already,' she laughed. 'I'm sure everyone can tell.'

'You look glowing,' I told her.

Thankfully she was feeling better. The sickness had started to subside and she was looking forward to her twelve-week scan the following week.

'I can't wait to see the baby on the screen,' she said with a smile. 'I know they say it's too early to tell whether it's a boy or a girl but I'm going to be looking really closely to see if I can spot anything.

'Charlie's got the morning off work and then we're going to go for lunch afterwards.'

She was bubbling with excitement and it was lovely to see her so happy. It was a welcome distraction from worrying about everything that had been happening here.

'How's Halima doing?' Louisa asked, as if she could read my mind.

I shrugged.

'Not great,' I sighed. 'School has been really hard for her.'

I thought back to her first day a few weeks ago when I had walked back to my car with tears in my eyes. It wasn't like me to have a wobble, particularly with a teenager of Halima's age, but I'd been consumed with a gut-wrenching anxiety. I'd dropped Halima off with Mrs Savage, who seemed lovely and had spoken to her reassuringly in Arabic, but I'd seen the look of utter fear in Halima's eyes. I'd put my hand on her shoulder and tried my best to calm her down, but she'd looked so scared and alone and so small in this huge, noisy comprehensive.

She'll be fine, I'd told myself as I drove away, but I couldn't control the knot of worry in my stomach.

I knew going to school was the best thing for her. She needed some routine, to meet teenagers her own age and to be submerged in the culture so she could start learning English. To my surprise, Ms Hicks had been right about her spoken English. Within a matter of days, Halima had started picking up basic words and we could almost have a conversation now without always having to rely on hand gestures or pointing. Every day she seemed to learn and understand more. It was incredible really.

'The school have been great but I can see it's tough for her,' I sighed.

Understandably she struggled to use written English so that made her feel very isolated in lessons. Mrs Savage had been helpful in getting her settled, but she had her own job to do and couldn't sit with Halima in every subject. She was very sweet and called me with regular updates. She'd tell me if Halima had had a good or a bad day, and if Halima wanted to, Mrs Savage would let her come and sit with her in the office at lunchtime and breaks if she needed somewhere to go. Unsurprisingly, it seemed that Halima was struggling to make friends because of the language barrier.

Natalie had been brilliant. She kept an eye out for Halima at school, but she was only eleven and I didn't want her to feel like the older girl was her responsibility.

'I feel so sorry for her,' sighed Louisa. 'She must be really homesick and miss her family and friends so much.'

'I'm sure she does,' I replied.

Not that any of us could know – Halima still hadn't talked about her family or her life in Iraq.

It was nice to have a catch-up with Louisa but I had paperwork to do, then I had a supervision session with my supervising social worker Becky in the afternoon.

'Good luck with the scan, flower,' I told her, giving her a hug as she left. 'Let me know how it goes.'

'I will.' She grinned. 'I can't wait to see him or her.'

I was looking forward to Becky coming round later. These sessions were a chance for us to catch up on how things were going with the children and for me to raise any issues or problems that I might be having. I'd worked for the same fostering agency for years so Becky and I had built up a good rapport. It was also a chance for Becky to pass on details of any support groups that might be useful or extra training.

'Let's talk about Natalie first,' said Becky, after I'd made us a cup of tea and we'd settled down at the kitchen table. 'How's she getting on?'

'Nat's doing really well,' I said. 'She's still going to visit Peggy three times a week after school but I know it's been really hard for her to see her deteriorating.'

I'd dropped Nat off one afternoon earlier in the week and I'd popped in to say hello. I hadn't seen Peggy for weeks and I was shocked by how much of a decline there had been in her health.

'She's in a wheelchair now and her speech has started to go, so she was slurring her words,' I sighed. 'It's just so sad.'

Peggy wasn't an old woman by any means, and it was awful how this cruel, devastating disease was slowly killing her.

'Does Nat talk to you about it?' asked Becky.

'Not really, but it's clear she finds it very upsetting,' I told her. 'She keeps a lot of it in. But I know she's happy at school, and she has plenty of friends so hopefully she talks to them.'

Then we moved on to Halima. I told her everything that I'd told Louisa. How hard school was proving to be for her and how she seemed very isolated.

'Has she said anything more about her family or getting to this country?' Becky asked.

'Sadly not,' I replied. 'But I deliberately haven't asked her. I talked about it with Penny and we decided to move away from pressing her to give us information before she's ready. It's hard enough for her to settle into school and having to learn a new language. I'm hoping that eventually, given time, she'll confide in me as her trust and her confidence in the language grows.'

I also wanted to talk to her about the fact that Halima was showing signs of someone who had gone through trauma, pacing her room all night long. At first when she had come to live with me, she was practically nocturnal. Gradually, because school had enforced some routine into her day, she was going to sleep a lot earlier, but she would still scream and cry out in her sleep and I would run in and check on her.

'I feel so powerless,' I explained to Becky. 'Without a shared language, it's hard to comfort her and make it any better.'

Although she was a teenager, I still treated Halima the same as any child having a nightmare. I gently woke her up and reassured her that she was safe. Even if she didn't understand what I was saying, I hoped that she would hear the comforting tone of my voice and be soothed.

'Do you think she would benefit from some counselling?' asked Becky.

'At this stage, I don't think so,' I sighed. 'I don't think she's ready to talk about anything just now.'

I explained that, from the little Arabic that I had learnt, Halima was shouting for her father in her sleep.

'She also calls out for someone called Muhammad,' I told her. But I had no idea who he was.

'It sounds like you're doing all the right things, Maggie,' Becky reassured me. 'And as Halima feels more settled and gets to grips with English, hopefully she'll start to open up to you more.'

I really hoped so.

*

A few days later, my phone rang. I recognised the school's number so I picked it up assuming it was Mrs Savage calling me with an update.

'Ms Hartley?' said an unfamiliar young woman's voice. 'This is Ellie Morgan. I'm Halima's art teacher.'

'Oh, hello,' I said, surprised. I had no idea why she might be ringing me.

'I wondered if you'd be able to come up to school as I'd like to have a chat to you about Halima?'

'Er yes, of course,' I replied.

I arranged to go into school that lunchtime and put the phone down, feeling puzzled. Why on earth did Halima's art teacher want to see me?

Later that morning, I drove to the school. Miss Morgan was waiting for me at reception. She was quite young and was dressed quirkily with bright red lipstick, chunky boots and lots of interesting jewellery.

'Thanks so much for coming in to see me,' she said.

She took me to the art block and as I walked into the class-room, I could see that one of the large tables was covered with an array of artwork. Some were paintings, others were charcoal or pencil drawings. They looked like they'd been done by someone extremely talented, and were very striking, but also undeniably disturbing and bleak. There were landscapes that looked like war zones, with piles of rubble and barbed wire, faces with their features scribbled out or contorted into screams. In one vivid charcoal picture, the floor was red with what looked like pools of blood and the sky was depicted as a crying face.

'Wow, these are very dark, but they're amazing,' I said, staring at the table of artwork.

'They're Halima's,' Miss Morgan told me.

'She did all of these?' I gasped, and she nodded.

'That's why I wanted you to come in,' she replied. 'I felt you needed to see them.'

I was totally and utterly gobsmacked.

'The work that Halima has produced in the past few weeks since she started here is incredible,' she added. 'I show her some examples and give her the materials and off she goes. The creativity just seems to pour out of her and it's like she's lost in her own world.'

I was stunned, not only by Halima's talent, but also by just how harrowing all of her pictures were.

'They're all so dark,' I sighed.

'In my teaching career I've found that art can be an outlet for children who have experienced trauma in their lives,' Miss Morgan told me. 'As Halima's carer, I felt you needed to see them as she's obviously in a lot of pain.'

As I looked through the pictures, I could see that an outlet was exactly what these were. It was as if I could see all of Halima's hurt and anger expressed on these pieces of paper.

This was her therapy. In every other lesson she was confined by her lack of language, but in art she was free to express herself and she'd certainly done that. It was hard to think that all of this was going on in her head and I had so many questions. Was this what had happened to her in Iraq? After all, she'd come from a country that had been torn apart by war, ever since the US and our own country had invaded and overthrown Saddam Hussein's government. Were these imagined situations or were they in fact very real?

'Would you mind if I took a few photographs of her work?' I asked. 'I'd like to show them to her social worker.'

'Yes of course,' Miss Morgan said.

I wanted to show them to Penny, and perhaps in time I could use them as a prompt to talk to Halima.

'She's such a brave young woman,' sighed Miss Morgan. 'I've seen such a change in her. At first, she would sit at the back of the class with her head down. She wouldn't put her hand up or talk to anyone. Now she'll make eye contact with me and attempt to have a conversation.'

It was a relief to hear that Halima was making some progress in her lessons, and that in art, at least, she had found a place where she could express herself.

'Thank you for showing me these,' I said. 'I can see by her work that Halima's really hurting and I'm glad she's got this outlet.'

'She's really talented.' Miss Morgan smiled. 'Every now and again pupils come along and blow you away with their skill, and Halima is one of those. Every lesson I look forward to seeing what she comes up with next.'

I really wanted to have the opportunity to talk to Halima about her artwork, but I didn't want to betray her trust and tell her that I'd been up to school to see them. I wanted her to show them to me of her own accord.

'I don't know how you'd feel about this but could you perhaps suggest that Halima brings one or two of these pictures back home with her?' I asked Miss Morgan. 'I'd love to talk to her about them but I think it might be better if she was able to bring it up herself.'

'Yes of course,' she told me. 'I can try.'

When I got home, I rang Penny and told her what had happened.

'What sort of pictures?' she asked, so I sent her some of the photos that I'd taken of them.

'Good grief,' she sighed. 'They're very bleak and gruesome.'

'I think Halima has found her own form of therapy,' I told her.

I explained that I'd asked the art teacher to get Halima to bring some of her work home, and she agreed that it would be a good opportunity to try and talk to her about her experiences, and what the pictures signified.

I was constantly looking for ways to bond with Halima. Due to the language gap, we couldn't play a game, watch a film or go to the cinema together and she didn't seem that interested in clothes or shopping.

Baking was always a good shared activity that I found both children and teenagers enjoyed. We hadn't seen Emaa since we'd gone round for dinner a few weeks ago but she'd kept in touch to see how Halima was getting on.

That afternoon I gave her a ring.

'Maggie, you were just on my mind,' she told me when I called her. 'I've been wondering how everything is going with Halima and school?'

I gave her a quick update.

'I wanted to do some baking with her and I thought it would be nice if we made some traditional Iraqi food together,' I told her. 'I thought you might be able to suggest something and have a recipe that we could use.'

'What a lovely idea,' she replied. 'And I know just the thing. You could have a go at making kleicha.'

She explained that kleicha were Iraqi date cookies traditionally eaten at birthdays and other family celebrations.

'Every Iraqi will have had kleicha growing up,' Emaa told me. 'I'll email you the recipe.'

'They sound perfect and delicious too,' I replied.

Emaa kept to her word and I got all of the ingredients together to make the date biscuits. On Saturday afternoon I dropped Natalie off at a friend's house for a party and then Halima and I headed home.

'I've got a surprise for you.' I smiled. 'You and I are going to do some baking.'

Halima looked at me blankly.

'I'm sorry I do not understand,' she told me.

It was one of the phrases that she had picked up very quickly at school so she could let the teachers know if she was having problems.

'We're going to make some cookies,' I said, getting out the scales, a bowl and a spoon.

'Baking,' I said, pretending to stir an imaginary mixture in the empty bowl. 'We're going to make kleicha.'

Halima's face instantly lit up.

'Yes.' She nodded. 'Kleicha. I know this.'

I'd printed out the recipe and I got the ingredients out and put them on the work surface. Halima, however, didn't need to follow the recipe; she instinctively knew what to do. I watched in amazement as she carefully measured out the flour and the cumin, fennel seeds and cardamom and proceeded to expertly make the fragrant pastry while the date mixture bubbled away on the hob.

'I can tell that you've made these before.' I smiled.

Halima nodded sadly as she rolled out the pastry. She'd got the consistency of the date mixture just right as she spread it on top of the layer of pastry with a palette knife. Then she carefully folded it up into one large roll.

'Perfect.' I smiled, giving her a thumbs up. 'You did that brilliantly.'

Half an hour later we'd cleaned up and I took it out of the oven triumphantly. I handed Halima the knife and got her to carefully cut the large roll into smaller cookies.

'You have the first one,' I said, handing her the tray.

She picked up a biscuit and took a bite.

'Good?' I asked and she nodded.

But as she chewed, she looked away and I suddenly realised there were tears in her eyes.

'What is it, Halima?' I asked her gently, putting my arm around her. 'Do these cookies remind you of home? Of Iraq?'

'Iraq?' she questioned. 'Yes.'

'My mother she make,' she sighed, pointing to the biscuits.

I held my breath. This was the first time that Halima had ever mentioned her family. There was so much that I wanted to ask her; however, I knew I had to tread very carefully here.

'Halima,' I said gently. 'Where is your mother? Is she at home in Iraq?'

She shook her head and looked down at the floor.

'She is died,' she told me. 'My mother is died.'

The words stuck in her throat and she collapsed into my arms and sobbed her heart out.

SEVEN

A Picture Paints a Thousand Words

Halima's frail body shook in my arms as she sobbed and sobbed.

'It's OK,' I soothed. 'That's it, let it all out.'

I could tell this was a huge emotional release for her and all I could do was hold her until the tears subsided.

When she was a little bit calmer, I got her to sit down at the table and I handed her some tissues.

'I'm so sorry about your mum,' I told her, putting my hand on hers.

'I am OK,' said Halima bravely, wiping her eyes.

'And I'm sorry if the baking upset you,' I told her.

She shook her head.

'No, I like,' she replied, giving me a weak smile. 'I love kleicha.'

'Did it make you feel sad about your mother?' I asked gently and Halima nodded.

So many questions that I was desperate to ask her ran through my head but I could tell that she was exhausted. I also knew that if I bombarded her now there was a chance that she would never open up to me again. As today had proved, she would tell me in her own time.

That afternoon I dropped a quick email to Penny and Becky telling them what had happened.

Today Halima disclosed that her mum had died. She was very upset and she didn't give me any other details but at least it's a start.

Halima was very quiet and withdrawn and spent the rest of the day in her room. I checked on her from time to time but I understood that perhaps she needed to be alone with her thoughts for a while.

'What's wrong with her?' asked Natalie when she got in from her party.

'She's just feeling a bit sad,' I told her. 'I think she's missing her family.'

'That is sad,' agreed Natalie. 'I miss living with Nan.'

Her eyes filled with tears and I gave her hand a squeeze.

'You'll get to visit her tomorrow, lovey,' I told her.

Natalie was generally such a bright, happy-go-lucky girl, but I knew how hard it must be for her to see someone she loved so desperately ill. Peggy was her only family and every so often I would see flickers of sadness creep up on her. For someone so young, she'd dealt with so much.

That night, I went to bed with a heart heavy, thinking about these two girls both carrying such heavy loads for ones so young.

A few hours later, I woke up with a start to hear loud screaming. I was so used to it now I knew exactly where it was coming from.

Halima.

But that didn't stop my heart from thumping as I ran down the landing to her room. It was always so loud and gut-wrenching, as if something horrific had just happened and it never failed to shock me.

Halima was sitting up in bed but I could tell from the vacant, glassy look in her eyes that she was still asleep. Her brow was covered in sweat and tears ran down her face. She whispered something over and over again as she gently sobbed.

'Mama,' she wept. 'Mama.'

This time I didn't need a translator to tell me who she was crying for.

'Oh, Halima,' I said as I gently shook her awake. 'It's OK. I'm here.'

'Mama?' she said, confused, as she opened her eyes and saw me.

Reality kicked in a few seconds later as she came to and remembered where she was.

'You must really miss her,' I told her, putting my hand on hers.

I don't know whether Halima understood or not but she lay back down and turned away from me, curled up protectively in the foetal position.

'Night night, sweetie,' I whispered.

I hoped that she was so exhausted after today that she would quickly nod back off. But I couldn't get back to sleep, no matter how hard I tried. I kept thinking about Halima and her poor mother and wondering what had happened to her. Was her father dead too? Perhaps that's why she didn't want to tell us about her family because she didn't have one any more.

I knew many of the unaccompanied minors who came to Europe were often orphans whose parents had been killed in conflicts and war. She must feel so utterly alone and my heart broke for her.

On Monday morning, when the girls were back at school, I called Penny for a catch-up.

'I saw your email,' she sighed. 'Poor Halima. Did you ask her about anything else? Did she say how her mum had died?'

'I wanted to, but she was so upset, it just didn't seem right,' I told her. 'I'm not sure that she has the words yet either.'

I also phoned Mrs Savage at school to tell her what had happened in case Halima seemed particularly low or anxious this week. I spent the rest of the day churning it over in my mind, wondering what I could do to help her.

Thankfully that afternoon when I went to pick her and Natalie up from school, she seemed OK. We'd only been home for five minutes when there was a knock at the door. I opened it to find a beaming Louisa standing on the doorstep.

'I brought you a present,' she said, handing me an envelope.

Puzzled, I walked through to the kitchen with Louisa following close behind.

'Go on,' she encouraged me. 'Open it.'

The girls watched curiously as I ripped open the envelope. When I saw what was inside, I gasped.

'Oh my goodness,' I cried.

In my hand was a grainy black-and-white scan photo. In all of my worry about Halima, I'd completely forgotten that Louisa's twelve-week scan had been today.

'That's a funny photo,' said Natalie, looking over my shoulder at the image in my hand.

'It's a baby.' Louisa smiled. 'My baby.'

'Oh, you've got a baby in your tummy?' asked Natalie. 'Wow, that's really cool they can take a picture of it in there.'

'It is, isn't it,' I laughed.

'Is it a boy or a girl?' she asked.

'It's too early to tell,' Louisa told her. 'But I think it's a boy. I just have a feeling.'

Halima looked on intrigued.

'Louisa's having a baby,' Natalie told her, pointing to Louisa's stomach.

'OK.' She smiled, giving a thumbs up. 'Good.'

'He or she is absolutely perfect,' I told her. 'You can start telling people the good news now.'

'I know,' she agreed. 'Although to be honest, I've been so excited I've told most people already, although I'll probably put it on Facebook now.'

They'd even picked out names – Dominic or Ethan for a boy and Joy or Millie for a girl.

It was a nice distraction after what had been a sad couple of days in our house.

Halima had been with me for six weeks when it was time to have a review meeting. An awful lot of foster care is about meetings and paperwork, and although I didn't think there was a huge amount to say in this case, it had to take place so that the box could be ticked. The aim of a review was to talk about what had happened and to come up with a plan of what was best for the child going forward.

As Halima was at school, it was held at my house. I looked around my living room, which was full of people. Penny was there as well as Becky and Ms Hicks, Halima's head teacher. Fatima was also there as she had spent quite a bit of time translating for Halima so her input was valuable too. A woman called Lydia had been appointed as the independent reviewing officer, or IRO as they were known. She was someone who worked for Social Services but who wasn't involved in this case and could make sure Halima's interests were being met. She was a very no-nonsense, professional woman.

Lydia led the meeting and she summarised what had happened so far.

'So, as we all know, Halima is a refugee from Iraq and arrived in this country as an unaccompanied minor,' she recapped. 'She was found barefoot at a petrol station trying to get into the back of a lorry while the driver was paying for his fuel. We still don't know how long she had been in the UK or how she got here. We do think it had been days and that she had possibly been sleeping rough.'

Hearing all of that made me realise how far she had come from that frightened shell of a girl who had arrived on my doorstep six weeks ago. Sometimes it felt as though we were wading through treacle and hadn't got any further, but in reality, Halima had started to make brilliant progress. She was speaking more and more English every day, going to school and settling into a routine. I really hoped she felt safe and supported, though it was hard to tell.

'It's very difficult to know how to move forward because we still don't have any significant history,' said Penny. 'Halima has disclosed recently to Maggie that her mother is dead but we don't know the whereabouts of her father or if she has any other family members in the UK.

'Everything has been very slow to start with because we've had the language barrier to contend with and we've had to rely on translation, but luckily this is getting easier the more Halima learns.'

Then it was Ms Hicks' stime to talk.

'How has Halima been at school?' Lydia asked her.

'She has settled OK,' she told us. 'She's coming in every day. I know from talking to her teachers that she's still very shy and quiet in class and there hasn't been much interaction with her peers.

'Her lack of language is a barrier both to her learning and to her ability to make friends, but her spoken English has improved rapidly in the past few weeks.'

When it was my turn, there wasn't a huge amount that I could add.

'The language barrier has been a challenge and frustrating at times but I've just done what I can,' I sighed. 'In a way Halima's no different to any other child in care in that she needs to feel loved and cared for, to have stability and routine, so that's what I've been focusing on.'

My hope was that even if she couldn't understand English, she would still understand love.

'My one big hope is that, going forwards, she'll start to open up to us about where she's come from and her journey here to the UK. Then we can support her as well as we can and work out the best solution.'

'How do you think Halima has adapted to life in the UK?' Lydia asked. 'Every culture has its own nuances and I wondered how she was coping?'

'OK, I think,' I replied. 'We had an issue around sanitary towels but that was because of the language breakdown and we haven't had a repeat of that problem.'

'What about getting around?' she added. 'Getting the bus and managing money?'

To be honest, they were things I hadn't looked at yet. I drove Halima to school and walked her into the building and her meals were paid for at school by scanning her pass at the till.

'We've made Iraqi food together and we also have a friend who is from Iraq so we've spent time with her and her family. Halima really seemed to connect with them and she appeared very relaxed there.'

'Good.' Lydia nodded. 'We should keep on doing as much as we can to learn and understand about where she has come from.'

At this stage, there wasn't an awful lot that we could say about Halima's long-term future.

'We'll just have to wait and see,' sighed Lydia, closing her notes. 'I'm satisfied that we're doing all we can for Halima. We just have to hope that she'll start giving us some more information so we can work out what's best for her in the long run.'

It was frustrating but that's all we could do for now.

I knew Lydia had been right about getting Halima accustomed to life in the UK, and I knew it was important that she learn about our currency. I tipped out my purse one weekend and went through each coin and note with Halima, teaching her what each one was. It was a bit like when children were small and you were trying to teach them the value of money. If we were in a shop, I'd get Halima to look at the label and show me the coins that she would need to buy that item.

One afternoon, we went into the chemist's where Natalie saw some hair slides that she wanted. Social Services gave children in care a certain amount of pocket money each week, so Halima was able to save up for things she wanted.

'Can I have also?' Halima asked, pointing to the hair slides.

'Yes.' I nodded. 'You can use your pocket money and then go and pay for them.'

At the till, Halima got out her purse.

'That'll be £3.50 please,' said the cashier.

She rummaged nervously in her purse, struggling to find the right money.

'Look, you've got a pound there,' Natalie told her.

But I flashed her a look that said let her do this on her own.

Eventually Halima handed her three pound coins and a fifty-pence piece and the woman at the till gave her the receipt.

'You did it,' I told her, smiling. 'Well done.'

Halima looked relieved.

Even a simple task like paying for something in a shop could feel quite daunting when you weren't used to the coins.

'She's from Iraq,' Natalie told the shopkeeper as we left. 'That's why she doesn't know.'

It was another box ticked and something else Halima had achieved that would hopefully help build her confidence.

It was a usual afternoon after school. Natalie was sprawled out in the living room watching TV and Halima was sitting at the kitchen table doing homework.

'Do you mind if I get your PE kit out of your bag and put it in the wash?' I asked her.

Halima nodded.

But as I fished the drawstring bag out of her rucksack, I noticed I'd pulled two pieces of paper out with it.

'Oh, what are these?' I said aloud.

As I pulled them out, I realised that it was two of Halima's charcoal drawings that I'd seen at school. Miss Morgan must have given them to her to take home. One depicted the rubble, barbed wire and pools of blood. The other was of people running, screaming and crying, their faces contorted in distress.

'Wow,' I gasped. 'These are amazing. Did you do them?'

Halima nodded shyly.

'They're very good but so sad,' I told her, pointing to the picture and giving a thumbs up, then making a sad face.

'Is this home?' I asked, pointing to the pictures. 'Iraq?'

Halima nodded.

'You're really talented,' I told her, smiling. 'You should show these to Emaa when we go there.'

Emaa had invited us for dinner again the following evening.

'Do you think she would like?' Halima asked.

'Oh definitely.' I nodded.

When we went round the following day, Halima kept to her word and took the pictures with her. After dinner, I insisted on tidying up, so Emaa and Halima went through to sit in the living room.

'Halima, why don't you show Emaa your artwork?' I suggested.

'Halima has done some amazing drawings of Iraq,' I added.

'Oh definitely.' Emma smiled. 'I'd love to see them.'

Halima went to get them and they lapsed into Arabic. I left them deep in conversation while I went back into the kitchen and started to tackle the mountain of dirty dishes.

Fifteen minutes later, I'd loaded the dishwasher and had just finished scrubbing the pans when Emaa came into the kitchen.

Her face looked deadly serious.

'Is everything OK?' I asked her, surprised.

'Maggie, Halima would like to talk to you,' she told me. 'She said she's ready to tell you how and why she came to this country.'

EIGHT

The Most Dangerous Journey

As I walked into the lounge, Halima was sitting on the sofa clutching her drawings.

Paul had taken the children upstairs to bed so we had the room to ourselves. Emaa and I sat down either side of her.

Halima said something to Emaa in Arabic and she nodded.

'Maggie, Halima says she's ready to talk to you,' Emaa told me. 'She wants to tell you about Iraq and why she left.'

I gave Halima's hand a squeeze.

'If you're ready then I'm listening,' I said to her.

Emaa explained that it would be easier for Halima to tell her story in Arabic and she would translate for her.

'I understand.' I nodded.

'My family,' started Halima. 'I tell you about my family.'

'Yes,' I said. 'Please tell me about your family.'

My heart pounded out of my chest as I waited for her to begin. We were finally going to get what I'd been waiting for for the past two months – and that was answers.

Halima began to speak in Arabic and Emaa relayed it to me in English.

'Life was good in Baghdad,' she started. 'We were a happy family. We had a house and a car and my dad had a good job as a radiographer at the local hospital. Me and my older brother Muhammad went to school every day.'

I nodded.

'Then the men come and it is very bad,' said Halima, lapsing back into English.

'This is what they did,' she hissed angrily, pointing to her drawings.

She explained how it became unsafe to go outside. She described the bombs going off and seeing people being shot.

'One day on her way to school, she saw a pile of dead bodies just lying in the street,' said Emaa, repeating what Halima had told her.

Halima did an impression of someone holding a gun.

'They shot,' she said matter-of-factly. 'Blood on the floor. Big red pools everywhere.'

'Oh, Halima,' I gasped. 'That's horrific.'

I couldn't imagine how terrifying it must have been to live your daily life surrounded by such horrors, epecially as a child.

'You see,' she said, pointing again to the picture that she held in her hands. '*This* is Baghdad. *This* is what they did.'

Suddenly everything that she had drawn in her pictures made sense: the barbed wire, the pools of blood, people screaming and crying. And worst of all, what I'd thought was a pile of rubble was actually a heap of dead bodies.

These horrors were real. This had actually happened.

'So many bombs,' sighed Halima. 'Boom, boom always. All day and night. They hit the houses and blow up cars and then one day . . .'

Suddenly the words stuck in Halima's throat and she couldn't go on. I could see tears welling up in her eyes.

'One day Mama . . .'

I put my arm on her shoulder to reassure her.

'Is that what happened to your mother, Halima?' I gently asked her.

She nodded.

She took a deep breath and started to speak in Arabic again. Her voice wobbled with emotion as she struggled to get the words out.

'One morning her mother was walking to the market,' translated Emaa. 'Halima and Muhammad had just said goodbye to her. Just as she walked around the corner, a car bomb went off.'

'We hear loud noise,' added Halima. 'Boom! I screamed then I ran. Muhammad ran. Alarms were ringing. So much smoke. But it was too late, Mama was gone. So many people gone,' she sighed, shaking her head.

She paused.

'The bombs is bad because they cut you. They cut your body and the pieces go everywhere,' she said sadly. 'Legs, arms. I even see a head lying on the road. So much blood.'

Emaa wept openly as she heard all of this. I just felt shell-shocked at this unimaginable scene of horror.

'I'm so, so sorry, Halima,' I told her.

I put my arms around her and she nestled into my shoulder and sobbed. I couldn't even begin to imagine what she had been through. It was just horrific.

'I'm worried this is all too much for you,' I told Halima. She was distraught and I could see Emaa was upset too.

'I think we should have a little break.'

Emaa went to make us all a cup of tea and I fetched Halima a tissue.

'If it's too upsetting you don't have to go on if you don't want to,' I told her. 'I know this must be so hard.'

I wasn't sure if she understood what I was saying but she seemed to.

'No,' replied Halima defiantly, drying her tears. 'I want to tell you.'

'OK,' I told her, holding her hand. 'I'm listening.'

'Mama has gone and I cry every night,' she sighed. 'I so sad.'

I didn't think things could have got any worse but somehow they did. She described how a mortar had struck a nearby house, killing their neighbours. It was too dangerous for her to even go to school. I couldn't imagine what it was like to experience terror and violence like this on a daily basis.

Halima told us how people were being attacked for working with the government or with the Americans or British. People were wrongly accusing her father of being a translator for the government and he received death threats.

'Her father knew it wasn't safe in Iraq any more and he was worried that she and Muhammad were going to get hurt too,' explained Emaa. 'So he wanted them to leave the country and head to Europe.'

He gave them all of his savings in case they needed to pay people to help them across borders.

'One night there is a knock on the door,' said Halima. 'The soldiers they come to arrest my father for working for the Americans. He whispers to Muhammad and tells us to run.

'So we go. We run into the dark and we leave my father to be taken by the soldiers and we don't know whether we will ever see him again.'

Halima started to cry at the memory. In the space of just a few months, she'd lost her home and both of her parents.

Muhammad was twenty-one – six years older than Halima. And so, scared and alone and walking away from everything they had ever known, the pair had started their epic journey that would last almost eight months and take them over land and sea. I could barely comprehend it – they were literally fleeing for their lives.

I listened in awe as Halima described how they had travelled across Iraq on foot to the Turkish border. They had tried to keep moving and slept wherever they could, sometimes out in the open in the freezing cold, huddled together, often going without water or food for several days. They lived in fear of being attacked or shot. They didn't have passports or visas so they had paid someone to smuggle them across the border into Turkey.

They'd then travelled to the Turkish coast in the hope that they could get on a boat across the Aegean Sea to reach one of the Greek islands.

'So many desperate people and not many boats,' sighed Halima.

They had to sleep in a forest for three days with no food or water while they waited to get on a boat.

'I was so scared,' sighed Halima. 'Muhammad said it was only one mile but I knew it was very dangerous and many people had died.'

As she described the treacherous crossing, tears stung my eyes as I imagined the fear she must have felt.

They had to cross at night so they would be less likely to be seen and around forty of them crammed onto a flimsy inflatable dinghy.

'The waves were so big and I was so scared,' she said, her dark eyes welling up again at the terror of the memory. 'I was crying and holding Muhammad's hand.'

I held my breath as Halima told us how they had hit a rock and the dinghy punctured and started to sink. People were crying and praying as men, women and children fell into the icy water.

'I close my eyes and prepare to die,' muttered Halima. 'Water went over my head and I sink under and choke.'

Miraculously she was pulled from the sea by the Greek coastguard and taken to the mainland.

'What about Muhammad?' I asked her. 'Was he saved too?'

Halima's face fell and she shook her head.

'I cannot see him in the dark,' she sighed. 'I do not know where he is. I shout and shout for him but the water is too big. I do not know if he is alive or dead,' she mumbled, tears streaming down her face.

'Oh, Halima,' I sighed. 'I'm so sorry.'

Now Halima was totally and utterly alone. She'd spent the next few months on the Greek mainland in a makeshift camp for other refugees. There were rivers of mud and piles of rubbish everywhere and no running water or electricity.

She had to make her own shelter out of bits of plastic that she had found. Crime and disease was rife and as a lone young woman she was constantly scared of being attacked or raped. It sounded horrendous.

'I too frightened to sleep at night,' she told us. 'So I sleep in the day when the sun is out.'

That explained why she had practically been nocturnal when she had arrived at my house. In the makeshift camp she got friendly with a young French charity worker who spoke Arabic and had taken Halima under her wing. Eventually she had agreed to help her get to France.

The journey took five days, Halima lying in the back seat of the car under a blanket or in the boot as they drove from country to country, terrified of being discovered. The charity worker dropped her off in Calais where she spent a few days sleeping rough. Halima described how she had removed her headscarf so as not to draw attention to herself, which is what her brother had told her to do.

'So you *are* Muslim?' I asked and Halima nodded.

After a few days in Calais, unbeknown to the driver, she managed to sneak into the back of a lorry, which brought her to England. At the service station she had crept out to go to the toilet and the driver had caught her trying to get back in.

'So this is how I came here,' she told us. 'This is how I come to your house.'

Emaa and I looked at each other, completely shell-shocked. Neither of us could comprehend what Halima had been through and had had to endure.

'You poor, poor thing,' I told her, giving her a hug. 'You're safe now.'

Her body felt so frail in my arms.

'Halima, do you know where your father is?' I asked her. 'Is he still in Iraq?'

Her brow creased and she shook her head.

'I do not know what has happened to him,' she sighed.

She didn't have a mobile phone and she hadn't had any access to a computer, so he would have had no way of contacting her even if he was able to.

I was so glad that she had finally opened up to me but I could see that she was drained, both emotionally and physically. When she went off to the toilet, Emaa and I looked at each other.

'My goodness,' I sighed, shaking my head. 'How can one child go through so much?' In my lifetime I had never experienced such suffering or seen the things she had.

'It's just unbelievable,' agreed Emaa. 'The things she's seen are just horrendous.'

As we left, Emaa gave Halima a huge hug and said something to her in Arabic.

'Thank you for telling us your story,' she told her. 'Come round again soon, OK?'

Halima nodded.

'This is for you,' Halima said, handing her one of her drawings.

'Are you sure?' asked Emaa. 'These are your memories.'

'I want you to have it,' she said.

We drove home in silence, each of us lost in our own thoughts. Everything Halima had told us was still going round and round in my mind.

When we got home, Natalie had just got back from Peggy's.

'Is Halima OK?' she asked me. 'Her eyes are all red like she's been crying.'

'I am sad,' Halima told her.

Natalie, bless her, rushed over to her and put her arms around her. I thought it might be too much for Halima but she hugged Natalie back.

'Yes, I am very sad,' she sighed.

I could see Halima was exhausted so she went straight up to bed. Ten minutes later, I went to check on her. She was lying on her bed, looking at the old photograph – one of the only things that she'd brought with her.

'Is that your mum and dad?' I asked her and she nodded.

'And this,' she told me, pointing to the little boy stood next to her, 'this is Muhammad.'

'You must miss them all so much,' I sighed and she nodded sadly. 'You're very brave,' I added, giving her a cuddle.

I got up and walked towards the door.

'Night night, flower,' I told her.

As I turned off the light, I heard her voice ring out in the darkness.

'I like your house, Maggie,' she told me. 'Your house is safe.'

'Good.' I smiled. 'I'm glad you feel safe here.'

I sat downstairs with Natalie for a while and after she had gone to bed, I turned on my computer. I felt exhausted but I knew I needed to send an email to Penny and Becky while everything was still fresh in my mind. Even as I typed out everything Halima had shared, I still felt shocked and horrified by what she had been through. It was much, much worse than any of us had ever imagined. It was frankly a miracle that she had made it to the UK alive.

But where were her father and her brother? Were they still alive and how on earth could we find out what had happened to them?

After I'd turned off my computer, I ran myself a hot bath. I didn't think I would be able to sleep; my head was racing with all of the things Halima had told me. It was her trauma, but I was haunted by the images that she had described to us. A car alarm went off outside earlier and I had jumped up in shock, my ears ringing with the sound of an imaginary bomb. When I closed my eyes, all I could see was a dusty pavement stained with blood and body parts scattered across the ground.

Three months later . . .

NINE

Ordinary Girl

ABBA blared out from the kitchen and as I walked in, I was greeted by a mini disco.

Natalie and Halima had raided the dressing-up box and put on some pink and blue wigs and were dancing around, singing to 'Dancing Queen'. Halima didn't know any of the words so she was mainly humming but Natalie, who was clutching an inflatable microphone, certainly did.

'Look at you two,' I laughed. 'You didn't tell me we were doing karaoke tonight.'

'This is my nan's favourite song.' Natalie smiled. 'She always used to love getting up and having a dance to it.'

'Me too.' I smiled. 'I love a bit of ABBA.'

Peggy was very poorly. Her speech had almost completely gone but she was battling on with the help of a live-in carer.

Halima had been with me for five months now, and she was a different girl from the terrified one who had arrived on my doorstep. Her spoken English continued to improve and we could have full conversations now. She still struggled at school and her written English was a much slower learning process, but I was so proud of the progress that she had made and how hard she tried.

She was still shy and quiet but as her language had improved, I could see flickers of her personality coming through as she was more able to express herself.

'Girls, will you please set the table for me?' I asked them. 'Louisa will be here soon.'

Charlie was away, so she was coming round for dinner.

'What is our meal?' asked Halima.

'I'm doing a roast chicken,' I told her.

Halima looked puzzled.

'I'm sorry,' she told me. 'I do not understand.'

'You know chicken, you've had it loads of times before,' I told her, but Halima still looked blank.

'Chicken,' I said.

In desperation, I resorted to miming like I had in the early days when she'd just arrived. I started flapping some imaginary wings and moving my head as if I had a beak and was pecking the ground. Halima and Natalie dissolved into fits of laughter as they watched me clucking up and down the kitchen.

'Oh, Maggie, you're so funny,' laughed Natalie.

I realised then that I'd been had.

'You two are very mean,' I muttered, pretending to be cross. 'I think I do a very good chicken impression, thank you very much.'

Halima giggled. It was a lovely thing to hear as there hadn't been much laughter in the beginning. It was also lovely to see how much her and Natalie's relationship had developed now they could communicate with one another. Even though Natalie was four years younger, they had become good friends.

Ten minutes later, Louisa arrived.

'Ooh it smells lovely in here,' she said, lowering herself down gently onto a chair. 'I'm starving.'

She was five months' pregnant now, and had a prominent bump.

'How are you feeling, flower?' I asked her as she gave her burgeoning belly an affectionate rub.

'Great,' she said. 'I'm full of energy at the moment.'

She'd started shopping for baby things and she and Charlie were busy decorating their spare bedroom and turning it into a nursery.

'I've got a surprise for you,' I told Louisa after we'd finished eating dinner.

The girls both looked at me and smiled because they were in on the secret too. We all led Louisa to the living room where there was a huge box in the middle of the floor.

'Oh my goodness, Maggie,' she gasped. 'You've got me a pushchair.'

'It's not just a pushchair,' I joked. 'It's a travel system.'

'I love it,' she said, studying the box. 'It's the one we really wanted but we couldn't afford.'

'I know.' I smiled.

I'd remembered her showing it to me months ago in a catalogue and I'd made a note of it.

'I wanted to get you something for the baby and I knew money was tight,' I told her.

'Thank you so much,' she sighed, flinging her arms around me. 'This baby is so lucky.'

I offered to store the pushchair at my house until they'd finished their decorating. Louisa was also excited because they had their twenty-week growth scan in a few days' time.

'I'll come round later in the week and show you the pictures,' she told me.

It was lovely to see her so happy.

This week was also going to be a significant one for Halima as we had an appointment with a charity that ran a refugee tracing service for families who had been separated by war. Halima was desperately hoping to be able to find her brother and also get back in touch with her father in Iraq. She had passed on his mobile number and email address to Penny and she had tried them but they were no longer active.

Telling me and Emaa what she had been through in Iraq seemed to have provided a little bit of relief for Halima. But although I was happy that she'd finally opened up to us, I also knew that what she had experienced and seen was the kind of deep-seated trauma that would stay with her for the rest of her life.

That night at Emaa's, she had also revealed that she was a Muslim and it was really important to me to respect a child's culture and religion. I'd fostered Muslim children before so I knew quite a bit about it.

'I can get you a copy of the Koran and a prayer mat,' I'd told her. I also offered to go shopping with her for a hijab.

'We can go and have a look at the local mosque too, if you like,' I'd said.

However, Halima hadn't seemed interested.

'I don't think I want to wear a hijab any more,' she'd told me. 'I'm enjoying the freedom.'

She explained that in Iraq her father and Muhammad had gone to the mosque for prayers, but she and her mum were not allowed.

Food-wise I made sure that we didn't eat pork and I bought halal meat from the supermarket. Halima assured me that that was enough.

'I'm not sure I want to practise any more,' she told me. After everything she'd been through, I could see that she was questioning everything in her life.

I knew that, above everything else, the main way that I could help Halima was by providing her with a stable home life to come back to after school every day. After so much trauma, grief and upheaval in her life, the things she needed the most now were routine and security.

Art was still her therapy and although she didn't seem to want to do it at home, she was still throwing herself into it at school. At parents' evening, Miss Morgan had shown me some of the work that she'd been producing lately.

'She's moved on to sculpture because I felt paper or canvas wasn't enough for her,' she'd told me. 'Her hands want to continually keep moving.'

She'd given her clay and then bits of scrap and she'd produced these huge towering sculptures that looked like twisted metal. They were so striking and unusual. Whatever she was feeling inside was coming out in her artwork and it seemed to be a good outlet for her. However, Halima was still generally struggling at school. She'd found it hard to make friends and I knew she dreaded break times, so Miss Morgan let her come into the art room at lunchtimes to work on her projects.

Nothing had stopped the nightmares though. That evening, after we'd waved Louisa off and the girls had gone to bed, I was locking up for the night when I heard blood-curdling screams echoing from upstairs. I'd never known a child who could scream so loudly and continuously in their sleep and not wake themselves up. Sometimes she would scream and cry for her mother, other times she would desperately call out for her father. Tonight she was sitting up in bed shaking and shouting out in Arabic, her eyes wide with pure terror and panic.

'Halima,' I soothed, gently shaking her. 'You're OK. You're at Maggie's house.'

I hated waking her up. Each time, there was a split second where she would suddenly realise where she was and the past would all come flooding back.

'You're OK,' I repeated to her as I stroked her hair.

'Was it another one?'

She nodded.

'I thought I was back in Iraq and I was walking with Mama and I was begging her to go another way because I knew about the bomb,' she garbled. 'But I couldn't save her.'

'Oh, lovey, I'm sorry,' I told her, giving her a hug.

It must have been exhausting for her having to relive that every night.

As I walked to my bedroom, my only consolation, if you could call it that, was that now I knew what her nightmares were about, I could imagine some of the disturbing images that she had in her head.

I thought perhaps the appointment at the charity was preying on her mind. She wanted information about her family; however, she was also scared about what she might find.

Halima had the following morning off school so we could drive to the Refugee Family Reunion Service, which was based in a city about an hour away from my house. Ordinarily they spoke to people over the phone, but because Halima was a child, they had agreed to see us in person.

Penny came round to pick us up and I had a quiet word with her in the kitchen before we left.

'I think she's really anxious about today and what they're going to say,' I told her.

'They probably won't have anything to tell us today,' Penny replied. 'These things can take months and even then, they might not be able to find out anything.'

'And what if it's bad news?' I asked her. 'What if her brother didn't make it? What if her father has been killed?'

'Then at least Halima will know,' said Penny firmly. 'It's better than living in limbo.'

I wasn't sure how much grief and loss one child could take. She'd already lost her mother, and it was heartbreaking to think that her beloved brother could be dead too. Sadly I wasn't holding out much hope. If he had been rescued too, surely he would have been taken to the same refugee camp as Halima? There had been no word about her father either.

The woman at the charity was in her twenties and couldn't have been nicer. She'd worked with countless refugees and was very kind and gentle with Halima.

'First, I'm going to ask you some questions about your relatives,' she told us. 'Then your foster carer or social worker can help you fill out a form.'

She took some details about Halima's father Ahmed, asking Halima when she had last seen him, their home address, his work address, his email address and the last phone number that she'd had for him.

'If he got out of prison then he might have moved,' Halima told her. 'Perhaps he left Baghdad as it is too dangerous.'

She also told her about the last time that she had seen Muhammad. Although Penny had read the information in my email, she had never heard Halima tell the story in her own words and she was visibly shocked.

I could see Halima was very focused and this time she didn't break down as she described how the dinghy had capsized and they had all fallen into the freezing water. She also gave them a description of Muhammad.

'All we can do is start a search in both Greece and Turkey where he was last seen,' the woman told her. 'Hopefully like you he was rescued by someone and taken to the shore.'

'Do you have any photos of your brother?' she asked her.

'I have one but he was a boy,' she replied. 'He was only eleven.'

That was the photo that Halima had arrived with and that I'd since put in a frame for her next to her bed.

'When will you find them?' Halima asked her eagerly.

'I can't promise anything,' she told her gently. 'And I'm sorry to say that in the majority of cases, we don't ever get any information. But I will contact my colleagues in Baghdad, Turkey and Greece and let you know if and when we get any news. I'll also add you to our database and check in case your family are looking for you.'

Halima looked crestfallen but I agreed with Penny. Although it would be devastating for Halima to hear that her brother and father were no longer alive, it was important that she knew the reality rather than living with the false hope of a fairy-tale reunion. The reality was it was like looking for a needle in a haystack. Many refugees arrived in countries and deliberately slipped under the radar because they were there illegally.

All Halima had left of her family was that crumpled, faded photograph. I knew how much she treasured it so as well as putting it in a frame for her, I'd made a copy of it and sent it off to a place that printed it onto a piece of material.

Halima was there a couple of weeks later when the parcel arrived.

'Look at this,' I told her and when she saw the material, she grinned.

'I thought I would make it into a cushion for your bed.' I smiled.

A cushion was a lot more tactile than a crumpled photo. It was something soft and warm that she could cuddle and hold.

When I got my sewing machine out, Halima's face lit up.

'I used to do this with my mother,' she told me. 'Mama used to make all her clothes out of beautiful fabrics that she'd pick up.'

She described how outside the house she would have to wear an abaya – a traditional long, dark dress – but when she was at home she loved to wear brightly coloured dresses.

'She taught me how to sew and we'd make things together,' she said, smiling at the memory.

'Would you like to have a go?' I asked her and she nodded.

She knew exactly what to do and she expertly and confidently guided the material through the machine to make a cushion.

It hardly took her any time and she even managed to sew a zip into it.

After she'd finished, she rummaged in my box of scrap fabrics and picked out some beautiful green and purple silk which she edged the cushion with.

'These colours remind me of her,' she said sadly.

She seemed really pleased with it and the following day, when Natalie and Halima were at school and I was tidying up, I was happy to see the cushion had pride of place propped up on her pillow. All I could hope was that it brought her some much-needed comfort.

As I walked downstairs, I was lost in thought about Halima when suddenly I heard my mobile ringing in the kitchen. I dashed to answer it and I was surprised when I saw Charlie's number flash up. It was the middle of the day and he was normally at work. It was usually Louisa who phoned me and not him.

'Hi, Charlie,' I said. 'Is everything OK?'

'No, not really,' he told me. 'Please can you come round to the flat, Maggie?'

His voice sounded odd. Strained somehow.

'It's Louisa,' he said. 'She needs you. Something terrible has happened.'

In that single moment my heart sank and I grabbed my keys before dashing out of the door.

TEN

Empty Arms

I drove to Louisa's flat on autopilot. My stomach churned with worry and panic as I repeated the same thing over and over in my head.

Please don't let it be the baby. Please don't let it be the baby.

But when I saw Charlie's face as he opened the door to me, ashen and etched with worry, I knew that it was.

My heart sank.

'What's happened?' I asked him.

'We had the five-month scan and they said there's something wrong with the baby. They don't think it's going to live, Maggie.'

He didn't need to say any more. I dashed into the living room to find Louisa, her face puffy and her eyes red raw, pacing the floor.

'Lovey, I'm so sorry,' I sighed.

I tried to put my arms around her but she brushed me off and carried on pacing up and down.

'We need to find another doctor, Maggie,' she ranted.

'They've got it all wrong. There must be something they can do to save him.'

My heart flinched.

'Oh, it's a little boy?' I smiled.

Charlie nodded sadly. My heart ached for them as I knew how much Louisa had yearned for a son.

'You read about these things all the time, don't you?' she continued. 'The doctors make a mistake and then someone else comes along and says that they can help . . .'

'Louisa, they said they'd had specialists look at the scans and there was nothing they could do,' urged Charlie.

'Please come and sit down,' he begged her.

'I'm not sitting down,' she told him. 'I'm going to look online and find another doctor. Maybe we could go to America? I bet they've got loads of experts that could help us there.'

It was unbearable seeing her like this. I went over and took her hand.

'Come and sit down,' I told her gently. 'You're going to wear yourself out pacing like that.'

I led her to the sofa and to my relief, she sat down. I could see that she was in shock.

'Charlie, tell me what happened at the hospital,' I asked gently.

He described how they had gone for their twenty-week growth scan the day before.

'The sonographer said she'd spotted something that she wasn't happy about,' he explained. 'She thought there was something wrong with the baby's kidneys but she wanted to talk to her colleagues and for us to come back today for a specialist scan.'

'Oh, you poor things,' I sighed. 'Why didn't you call me?'

'We thought it would be OK.' Charlie shrugged. 'Louisa had read stuff about babies having operations in the womb or when they were born. We were worried but we convinced ourselves that, whatever it was, it was fixable and we just had to stay strong.'

Louisa sat next to me, staring into space, wringing a tissue in her hands.

'We went back today and saw a specialist and they agreed with the sonographer,' he continued. 'But it was much, much worse than we'd thought.'

He described how the scan had shown that their baby's kidneys, stomach and bowel hadn't developed properly and his heart was in the wrong place. They were told he had less than a one per cent chance of survival and that he probably wouldn't survive the duration of the pregnancy.

'What did they call it?' questioned Charlie. 'They said he was incompatible with life.'

On hearing this, Louisa let out a gut-wrenching howl.

'Oh, flower,' I whispered, tears streaming down my own face at seeing her in so much pain. 'I'm so, so sorry.'

'Do you think they've got it wrong, Maggie?' asked Louisa, standing up again. 'Do you think they've made a mistake?'

'Sweetie, I'm absolutely devastated for you but I think Charlie's right,' I told her gently. 'The doctors are experts in these kinds of things and they know what they're doing. I know it's a terrible thing to hear but it sounds like they've already got a second opinion.'

I didn't want to say it out loud but the prospects sounded very bleak.

I could see they were both in shock and I felt helpless. Charlie made us all a cup of tea while I sat with Louisa.

'I'm so angry, Maggie,' she wept. 'Why us? Why our baby? It's not fair.'

'No, you're right, it's not,' I sighed, rubbing her back.

'I can't bear it,' she sobbed. 'Even as they were telling us all this, I could feel him kicking me. He can't be dying if he's still moving around, can he?'

She started to cry again.

'So what happens now?' I asked gently.

'The doctors said they could induce her and then the baby would probably pass away during labour or straight afterwards,' replied Charlie. 'Or if we do nothing then they said he'll probably die anyway within the next few weeks or months.'

'How can I choose to end my baby's life?' sighed Louisa. 'I don't think I can do it, Maggie.'

'You have to make the decision that's best for you both,' I told her. 'And whatever you decide, you know that I'm here for you.'

I couldn't even begin to imagine what they were going through.

The hospital had given them a few days to work out what they wanted to do.

'Take all the time you need,' I said as I left. 'You know I'm here when you need me or if you want to talk.'

I hated leaving them in this state but I knew they needed space and time to talk about this as a couple and make their own decisions.

'Will you come and see me tomorrow, Maggie?' Louisa begged.

'Of course I will if you want me to,' I replied.

Charlie walked me to the door.

'Look after each other,' I told him and he nodded sadly.

'I'm so sorry this is happening,' I soothed as I gave him a hug.

On the drive home, I just felt numb. I managed to hold it together until I walked through the front door and saw the pushchair that I'd brought them standing in the hallway. I sat at the bottom of the stairs and wept.

My heart broke for Charlie and Louisa. They were so young; this was their first baby and it felt so unfair that they were having to go through this. I felt utterly helpless and I just wished there was something I could do to take some of their pain away.

I didn't know what to do with myself for the rest of the day. In an hour I'd have to go and pick Halima and Natalie up from school. I decided not to tell them anything at this stage – not until Louisa and Charlie had decided what to do. I knew the girls were going to be upset too, but for now, I'd have to put on a brave face.

Once again, I switched on to autopilot, cooking dinner, supervising homework and bedtimes, but all I could think about was Louisa.

When the girls were in bed, she rang.

'Maggie, it's me,' she said in a small voice. 'We've decided to go ahead and be induced. It's the hardest decision I've ever had to make but it's not fair on the baby. I don't think I can carry on being pregnant knowing that any minute his heart is going to stop beating and he's going to die. I don't want him to suffer or feel any pain.'

Charlie was going to phone the hospital tomorrow and put the wheels in motion.

'Oh, love,' I sighed. 'I don't know what to say. You're being incredibly brave.'

'I don't really have a choice,' she sighed.

That night I tossed and turned and hardly slept, going over the day's events again and again in my mind. After I'd dropped the girls off at school, I went round to see Louisa and Charlie. Charlie had just got off the phone to the hospital and they were going to go in later that day to be induced. Louisa was very scared and tearful.

'I don't think I can do it, Maggie,' she cried. 'I don't think I can give birth and go through all that pain and know that he isn't going to live.'

The other option was having a surgical termination but that meant they wouldn't be able to see or hold their baby.

'I don't even know whether I want to see him,' added Louisa. 'It might be too upsetting.'

'But remember what the lady at the hospital said,' Charlie told her. 'We might regret it if we don't. He's our little boy.'

There were so many horrendous, impossible decisions for them to make.

'You can do this,' Charlie said, squeezing her tight. 'I'll be with you every step of the way, holding your hand. And I'll make sure you get all the drugs.'

'Thanks,' she said, giving him a weak smile.

It was horrible, but I knew the two of them would get through this together.

Before I left, I gave Louisa a huge hug.

'I'll be thinking of you,' I told her. 'If you need me, you know where I am. You're a strong girl. You can do this, OK?'

She nodded tearfully.

Charlie followed me out of the front door.

'Maggie, when we're at the hospital, will you do me a favour?' he asked in a low voice. 'Will you come round and clear out all of the baby things from the nursery? Louisa has said she can't bear to come home from hospital and see them all there.'

'Yes of course,' I told him. 'I'll take it all home and keep it safe for you.'

Later that day, Charlie texted me to let me know they were on their way to the hospital. For Louisa's sake, I desperately hoped it wasn't a long labour.

Before I collected the girls, I went back to their flat and let myself in with the spare key that I had. I took a deep breath and steeled myself as I walked into the nursery and looked around. I hadn't seen it for a couple of weeks and they'd created the most beautiful room for their baby. Even though they'd still had a few months to go, everything was ready. The walls were painted in a light grey colour and there was a Miffy mobile and a matching Miffy print on the wall. The crib had been put up and there was an array of soft toys in it. A chest of drawers was filled with little sleepsuits and vests and even a tiny pair of white trainers. They'd got a change table with wicker baskets filled with nappies and creams and a car seat ready to take to the hospital. With a heavy heart, I packed it all away and loaded it into my car. It felt so wrong, and by the time I'd finished, the room looked so empty and bare.

The rest of the day dragged. Every few minutes, I checked my phone for news and wondered how Louisa was getting on but I heard nothing. After another sleepless night, it was just starting to get light when my phone buzzed with a text.

Our beautiful son Dominic was born at 2.30 a.m. He lived for five minutes and we got to hold him. Louisa was amazing. He's perfect.

Tears stung my eyes and before I could type out a reply, my mobile rang. It was Louisa. She sounded exhausted and shell-shocked.

'Oh, lovey, you have done so well,' I told her. 'I'm so, so proud of you.'

'He's beautiful, Maggie,' she told me.

She told me how they'd given him a bath and dressed him and read him a story. They'd taken lots of photographs and made prints of his tiny hands and feet.

'If it's OK with you, Maggie, we'd like you to come up to the hospital in a few hours to meet Dominic and say goodbye,' she told me. 'Charlie's parents are coming up later on.'

'It would be an absolute honour to meet my grandson,' I said, the words sticking in my throat.

I headed straight up to the hospital after the girls had left for school. Louisa and Charlie were in a special bereavement suite, which was thankfully separate from the main labour and maternity wards. The lighting was low and Louisa was sitting on the bed cuddling Dominic. He was wrapped up in a blanket and wearing the tiniest knitted hat that I'd ever seen. Louisa looked completely heartbroken but at the same time I could tell that she was so proud to show me her son.

Tears streamed down my face as Louisa gently passed me his tiny body. His skin was pink and so translucent that you could see his veins, but he was absolutely perfect.

'He's the most beautiful baby that I've ever seen.' I smiled.

'Hello, Dominic,' I told him, gently stroking his button nose with my finger. 'It's your nana here. We love you so much and you'll always be part of our family,' I whispered. 'We'll never ever forget you.'

I knew I'd remember those few precious moments with him for the rest of my life.

It was gut-wrenching handing him back to Louisa and walking out of that hospital knowing that I would never see him again. But I had to be strong for Charlie and Louisa. Louisa looked broken and I couldn't even begin to imagine how she was going to cope when it was their turn to say goodbye. But I knew this was something they wanted to do on their own.

That afternoon when I picked the girls up from school, I knew the time had come to tell them what had happened. When we got home, I sat them down in the kitchen.

I took a deep breath and did my best to compose myself. I wanted to try and get through telling them without breaking down.

'I'm afraid I've got some really sad news to share with you,' I sighed. 'Louisa and Charlie have had their baby – a little boy called Dominic. But he was very poorly and he had so many things wrong with him that sadly he died just after he was born.'

Both girls looked stunned as they took in the news.

Halima didn't know Louisa that well, but she looked devastated.

'That is very sad,' she said. 'I feel so sorry for them.'

Natalie just looked confused.

'I knew old people died but not little babies,' she sighed. 'That's not fair.'

'It's not.' I nodded. 'But sometimes life isn't fair and sadly these things happen.'

'The baby doesn't develop in the womb like it should do and no one knows why.'

'Poor Louisa,' said Natalie.

'She and Charlie are going to be very sad for a long time,' I told them. 'I know I feel very sad and upset about what's happened and you might too and that's OK. We can all feel sad together and I'm here to talk about it if and when you need to, OK?'

The girls nodded and I could tell that it would take them a bit of time to fully absorb what had happened.

Later that night, Charlie phoned.

'We're back home now,' he told me. 'Thank you for sorting out the spare room. I don't think either of us could have coped with coming home and seeing baby stuff everywhere.'

'How's Louisa?' I asked him.

'Heartbroken,' he sighed. 'She hasn't stopped crying.'

I asked him if she felt up to talking to me and he passed her the phone.

'I've been thinking about you all day,' I told her.

'I feel so numb and empty,' she sighed. 'It was so hard walking out of that hospital and leaving Dominic there.'

'I can't even imagine,' I told her.

'It wasn't meant to be like this, Maggie,' she sobbed. 'Why us? Why our baby?'

'I don't know,' I sighed.

It was awful knowing that there was nothing I could say or do to help them or take their pain away.

'The hospital gave us some leaflets and I think we're going to have him cremated. Charlie and I are going to go to the crematorium, just the two of us. I don't think I can cope with a big funeral.'

'You do what you need to,' I told her.

Despite everything that had happened to her as a child with the sudden death of her parents, Louisa had always been so upbeat. She always saw the best in everyone and everything and it was horrendous seeing her in so much pain. In a couple of days her whole world had been shattered and I knew that things were never ever going to be the same for them again.

ELEVEN

Finding Faith

As devastating as baby Dominic's death was, the old cliché was true – although we were grieving, life went on. For me, it had to. Natalie and Halima needed taking to school, there were meals to be cooked and cleaning to be done, doctors and dentist appointments, endless paperwork and meetings with school and Social Services. Everything was tinged with an aura of sadness though, and my thoughts were constantly with Louisa.

I rang her every day to see how she was. Some days she didn't even want to answer the phone. Other days she was desperate to talk and wanted to go over Dominic's birth and what he had looked like and all her memories of him. Before he was cremated, a post-mortem had been performed and it had found that what had happened to him wasn't genetic. It was one of those one in a million things and therefore wasn't likely to affect any future babies they might have. Knowing that seemed to provide some relief, but it also added to Louisa's sense of injustice and her endless wondering as to why such an awful thing had happened to them.

For a week after he was cremated, Louisa didn't get out of bed. Charlie, who was off work on compassionate leave, rang me in a state.

'She's hardly eating or sleeping and she just lies there crying,' he told me, his voice tinged with desperation.

'What should I do, Maggie?'

Unfortunately, I didn't have the answer.

'All you can do is talk to her and let her know that you're there for her, and hopefully she'll start to come round,' I told him.

'If you need me to come over, just let me know.'

I wanted to give them the space and time to grieve together.

After two weeks, Charlie had to go back to work but he was worried about leaving Louisa.

'I'll go round and check on her every day,' I reassured him.

On the first day I called in, she came to the door in her pyjamas. Her hair was unwashed and greasy and her face looked hollow with grief.

'How are you?' I asked, giving her a hug.

She shrugged.

'I don't know how I am any more,' she sighed.

She was still recovering from the birth, and cruelly her body was gearing up to care for a baby that had never made it home.

'The hospital gave me some tablets to stop my milk coming in but it's still been so painful,' she sighed. 'I feel so empty, Maggie,' she added. 'Mentally and physically.'

She was scared to go out in case she bumped into someone she knew and had to explain why she wasn't pregnant any more.

'When you feel ready, I'll go out with you,' I told her. 'We could just have a walk to the shops to get some fresh air.'

Little steps, that's all she could do.

'Anyway, how are the girls?' asked Louisa in a brave effort to change the subject. 'How's Nat's gran?'

'Peggy's still fighting,' I told her. 'She's very sick but she's hanging on in there. It's just such a terrible, slow decline.'

'And Halima?' she asked.

'Halima is OK,' I said.

In all honesty, I had been worried about Halima lately. Even though her English was brilliant, she was still very isolated at school. She didn't have any friends that I knew of and she never saw anyone outside of school. She was an outsider in all senses of the word. Not only was she new to the school, but her experience of life was totally different to everyone else's. She came from a different world to her peers and had been through things most of us were lucky enough to never have to face in our lifetimes.

That afternoon after I left Louisa's and had picked up the girls and taken them home, Natalie wandered into the kitchen. She hung around anxiously as if she had something on her mind.

'What is it, flower?' I asked her, thinking she wanted to talk to me about Peggy.

She hesitated, biting her lip and looking worried.

'It's Halima,' she replied eventually. 'I'm not being a snitch or nothing, but I saw some people being mean to her at school today.'

She described how it had happened in the canteen at lunchtime.

'They were making fun of her not being able to speak English properly and saying she couldn't sit with them.'

'That's awful,' I sighed.

'I don't think it's the first time people have said nasty things to her either,' said Natalie. 'They call her names and stuff. She's sad enough about not being with her family without people being mean to her.'

'Thanks for telling me, Nat,' I replied, giving her a hug. 'You're a good friend to her.'

That night when Natalie was in bed, I went to see Halima in her room.

'How are you doing, lovey?' I asked gently.

She shrugged, not meeting my eye.

'Nat mentioned that she saw some people being horrible to you at school today,' I went on.

'It happens many times,' she sighed. 'I get used to it. They make the fun of me for not speaking good English.'

'Would you like me to talk to the school about it?' I asked her. 'Because I think it's important that I do.'

She shook her head.

'It will not matter,' she sighed. 'They know I am not like them.'

But I was determined to say something. Even without everything she had already experienced, it was awful that children could be so cruel. I wanted to make it clear to her that this kind of behaviour wasn't acceptable.

Coincidentally, in a couple of days' time, I had a PEP meeting at Halima's school. PEP stood for Personal Education Plan and it was something Social Services put in place for every child in care to make sure that they were getting the best education they could at their school. A PEP meeting would be held every term at the school with myself, Penny, Ms Hicks and the head of pastoral care, Mr Granger.

The first thing that I raised at the meeting was my worries about Halima feeling isolated, and the name calling.

'I believe other pupils were making fun of her ability to speak English,' I finished.

'I do know that she has struggled to make friends,' said Mr Granger. 'And we will look into those allegations as that shouldn't be happening.'

We also talked about the fact that Halima still spent most of her break times in Miss Morgan's classroom doing art.

'Do you think perhaps we shouldn't give her that option and then she will have to mix with her peers rather than hiding away in the art room?' Mr Granger asked. 'That could actually be making her more isolated and preventing her from making friends.'

I felt torn. I knew Mr Granger had a point, but I also knew that the art room was Halima's safe haven.

'Art is so therapeutic for her and I know it's helping her to make sense of her past and process the trauma and grief that she's been through,' I told them.

'I agree.' Penny nodded. 'I think it would be detrimental to her mental health and it would cause her a lot of distress if we suddenly took that option away.'

We also discussed the difficulties Halima was still having with her written English.

'What her teachers have noticed is that she finds it easier to express herself when she has access to a computer rather than having to write longhand with pen and paper,' Ms Hicks told us.

'Could a laptop be something that Halima would benefit from?' asked Penny and she nodded.

'It would definitely be useful going forwards,' she replied. 'She could do her written homework on that, and potentially we could look at her using it in exams.'

Every child in the care system has a certain amount of money that can be spent directly on them by their school to help with their education, and this would cover a laptop.

'We can certainly look into getting that for her,' agreed Ms Hicks.

'In the meantime, I've got an old laptop that she could use until the new one is sorted out,' I suggested.

I was keen for us to do whatever we could to make things easier for Halima.

That evening I told Halima about the meeting and what had been decided.

'Mr Granger's going to look into the nasty comments those girls made, but if it happens again then promise me you will let me know,' I told her.

'OK,' she sighed.

'There was one bit of good news that I think you'll like,' I added. 'Social Services are going to get a laptop for you to use to do your schoolwork.'

'Laptop?' Halima replied, looking puzzled.

'Yes, your own computer,' I told her. 'A laptop is a portable one that you can carry around. You can take it to school and do your homework on it instead of having to write everything out.'

'Oh, yes, that would be good.' She smiled.

'Until the new one comes, I've got an old one that you can use,' I added.

She already had a desk in her bedroom and I knew she needed a quiet place to work so I set the laptop up for her in there.

'There you go,' I told her. 'Hopefully that will make things easier for you.'

She looked thrilled.

'I've never had a computer of my own before,' she said.

She took to it instantly. For the next few weeks, whenever she came home from school, she went upstairs and was on the computer working.

'How's it going at school?' I asked her one night. 'Have the nasty comments stopped?'

'For now,' she said. 'I am sure they will happen again.'

She seemed very weary with the social side of school.

One afternoon when I walked into her bedroom, I noticed that she quickly closed the laptop lid when I came in.

'What were you looking at?' I asked her casually.

'Oh, some maths homework,' she said.

However, I'd briefly seen the screen, which was all written in Arabic. I could tell by the guilty look on her face that it was something else and I had an inkling of what it might be.

'I think Halima's been trying to trace her father herself,' I told Penny.

I explained how when I walked into the room, she had hidden what she was doing from me.

'Well if she wants to try and trace him that way, I don't suppose there's a lot we can do about it,' she replied. 'I don't think she'll get very far though as the charity haven't got any leads.'

She had phoned them recently for an update and there was no information so far about Halima's brother or father. I had every sympathy for Halima. I could only imagine how desperate she must feel. She was terrified that her dad was still in prison, being mistreated, or worse, had been killed. I would have rather she went through the proper channels to try and find more information, but Penny didn't think there was much that we could do to stop her looking for him herself.

'How's the laptop working out?' Penny asked.

'Really well,' I told her. 'She's never off it.

'It really seems to have encouraged her with her schoolwork.'

All we could hope was that this would be the beginning of a more settled time for Halima and that she started to feel less isolated at school.

Several days later I was upstairs doing my most hated job – folding up clean washing into piles. I sorted out some of Halima's things and took them into her room so she could put them away. But when I knocked and walked in, she was lying on her bed crying.

'What on earth's the matter, flower?' I asked her, worried that something had happened at school.

'I am not a very good Muslim, Maggie,' she wept.

'What do you mean?' I asked, puzzled.

'I am not a good Muslim,' she sobbed. 'I missed Ramadan.'

I didn't know where all of this was coming from and I was confused. When Halima had first acknowledged that she was a Muslim some time ago, she didn't appear to be practising and had seemed to want to distance herself from her faith.

'Remember we talked about it a while ago and you said that you didn't want to wear a hijab or observe any of the Muslim traditions any more,' I gently reminded her.

'But I want to now,' she wailed.

119

Through her tears, she described how she wanted to start wearing a hijab again and a longer, looser skirt and a long-sleeved shirt for school.

'And I cannot have the school dinner because the food isn't halal,' she told me.

'Halima, I'm more than happy to support you in anything you want to do to honour your culture or your religion,' I replied. 'You just have to talk to me and tell me.'

'You don't care,' she snapped. 'You do not understand Islam.'

I was taken aback. It was the first time Halima had been cross with me.

'Halima, I know I'm not a Muslim myself, but I do try to understand Islam as best I can, both from you and other children that I've fostered,' I told her. 'But you need to tell me what you feel needs to happen in order for you to become a good Muslim. You need to teach me what Islam means for you, OK?'

She nodded and looked a little happier.

The following day after school we sat down and went through all of the things Halima wanted to do, which included wearing a hijab and more conservative clothing, praying daily and observing the Muslim calendar and feasts such as Ramadan.

A lot of it was going to need co-operation from the school.

'Let me talk to Penny and we'll organise a meeting with the school to discuss everything with them,' I told her.

She nodded.

I called Penny the following day.

'That's all absolutely fine, and of course we're happy to support her in her faith,' she said. 'Do you know why she's suddenly wanting to do all of this now? She didn't seem to be a particularly devout Muslim when she told us months ago.'

'I suppose in times of sadness or crisis or when you're feeling alone or vulnerable, people often cling to their faiths,' I suggested. 'I know she's still feeling very alienated at school and perhaps her faith offers her some comfort.'

With all the upheaval in her life, I supposed it made sense that she would turn to something familiar for some comfort. Islam was one connection to her past, and I could only assume that was what had brought about this renewed interest in her faith.

Before I had the meeting at Halima's school, I did some research of my own.

Children are asked to pray five times daily from the age of seven and they are required by Islam to do so from the time they reach puberty.

The prayers were at different times of the day, based around sunrise and sunset. In summer it meant that only one of the prayers would be in school time but now, as we were approaching winter, Halima would need to do three lots of prayers during the school day.

Thankfully Halima's school was very accommodating.

'We have two other Muslim pupils but neither of those boys have wanted to say prayers at school,' said Ms Hicks. 'But we can provide a quiet classroom for Halima to pray in. Do you know how long the prayers take?'

'From what I've read, no longer than ten minutes,' I replied.

Two of the prayer times could be taken at the beginning and the end of lunchtime.

'With regards to halal, we have a vegetarian option in the canteen every day.'

We also agreed that she could adapt the school uniform so it would fit in with her religious beliefs.

'She'd like to wear a tracksuit in PE and she won't be using the communal showers,' I told her. 'And for swimming she wants to wear a long-sleeved leotard and leggings in the water.'

'That's all absolutely fine,' Ms Hicks replied. 'If she needs anything else then just let us know.'

Like Penny, I was still curious as to where this newfound sense of religion was coming from. But if it gave Halima comfort then surely it had to be a good thing, and I was determined to support her 100 per cent.

TWELVE

Extreme Measures

My main aim now was to make sure that Halima felt like I was respecting and supporting her faith as it was clear how much being a Muslim meant to her. I read everything I could find about Islam and I also called Emaa and asked for her advice.

'Good for Halima if that's what she wants to do,' she told me. 'I grew up as a Muslim but I haven't practised for many years.'

She paused.

'It's funny though; Halima didn't strike me as someone who was a devout Muslim whenever we've talked about it.'

'That's definitely all changed in the past few weeks,' I told her. 'I must admit that it's surprised me too, but if it gives her some stability and comfort then that's a good thing and I'm trying to support her in any way that I can.'

Emaa told me about the shops that sold Islamic clothing in the area where Halima would be able to buy a hijab. So the following weekend I drove her there.

'I can go in alone,' she told me firmly as we pulled up outside.

'It's up to you,' I replied. 'Would you like me to come in with you?'

Halima shook her head.

'You would not know what to buy so I will go in myself.'

'You could show me,' I said in a bid to prove to her that I was interested in her faith and eager to learn more.

'No, I will go alone,' she insisted.

She seemed very determined and I had to respect that. Halima was used to English money by now, so I handed her some notes and she went into the shop.

Twenty minutes later, the shop door opened and Halima came out wearing a navy hijab that covered her head, neck and chest.

'Gosh, you look so different,' I said, as she got into the car. 'Are you all sorted?'

She nodded.

'There were many colours and patterns, but I chose plain blue and black ones because they look more modest,' she told me.

'Is it complicated to put on?' I asked her.

'Not when you know the technique,' she replied. 'There are lots of different ways to wrap it and then you secure it with pins. My mother taught me when I was younger.'

At the mention of her mum, I saw a flicker of sadness in her eyes.

'Did she wear a hijab?' I asked her and she nodded.

I put my hand on hers and gave it a squeeze.

'I bought three of them,' said Halima, pulling her hand away and quickly changing the subject. 'The woman said to wash them by hand instead of putting them in the washing machine as the fabric is very delicate.'

There was so much to learn that I hadn't even thought of.

When we got home, Natalie saw Halima and did a double take.

'Oh,' she said, sounding surprised. 'Why are you wearing that?'

'I'm a Muslim and the veil is something Muslim women wear,' Halima told her.

'But you didn't wear it when you first came here,' replied Natalie. 'You look weird.'

'Nat, Halima's headscarf is called a hijab,' I explained. 'And it probably looks weird to you because I'm assuming that you don't know anyone else who wears one?'

'Yeah.' She nodded. 'I've seen girls wearing them on TV but you're the first person in real life I know who wears one.'

Halima went upstairs and took the headscarf off.

'I don't need to wear it when I'm in the house,' she explained.

Later that afternoon, the girls were watching a film when there was a knock at the door. I was surprised to see Charlie standing there.

My heart sank.

'Is everything OK, lovey?' I asked him.

'I was just passing and I wanted to pop in to give you these,' he said, handing me a beautiful bunch of roses.

'I wanted to say thanks for everything you've done for us, you know, since Dominic . . .'

His voice trailed off.

'And thanks for looking in on Louisa while I've been at work.'

For the past few weeks I'd been calling in to see her every couple of days. I invited him in for a cup of tea.

'How's Louisa doing today?' I asked.

'Just the same,' he sighed. 'She doesn't want to go anywhere or do anything and she hardly leaves the flat.'

'Give her time,' I told him. 'She's grieving. You both are.'

We were chatting in the kitchen when Natalie and Halima walked in.

'Can we have a snack?' asked Natalie.

When Halima saw Charlie, her face fell. She gasped and ran out of the room.

'What's wrong with her?' asked Natalie, looking surprised.

'I'm not sure, flower, but I'm chatting to Charlie at the moment so I'll go and see her in a little bit.'

I waved goodbye to Charlie and promised to pop round and see Louisa later in the week. She was still entitled to maternity leave and hadn't been back to work since losing Dominic.

I was about to go upstairs and check on Halima when she wandered down. I noticed she was wearing her hijab now.

'Why have you got your scarf on?' asked Natalie. 'I thought you didn't wear it in the house?'

Halima glanced around, a confused look on her face.

'I put it on because Charlie was here,' she said. 'Muslims wear the veil to maintain modesty and privacy from the gaze of men who are not family.'

There was something about the way Halima was talking that sounded so strange. She sounded robotic, almost like she was repeating something from a book.

'He's gone now, lovey,' I told her. 'I'm sorry, I didn't realise he was coming round otherwise I would have told you.'

Charlie must have felt strange about what happened as he rang me later that day.

'Maggie, did I do something to upset Halima?' he asked. 'She seemed to be really uncomfortable having me in the house. Did she run off because of me?'

'Not at all,' I told him. 'She's started to wear a headscarf and I didn't realise that if a man visits who she isn't related to then she should be wearing her hijab.'

'Oh, I'm sorry I didn't know,' he said.

'Don't worry,' I told him. 'I didn't either. As I said to Halima, we're all learning.'

It was a continual learning curve. The following day, I managed to persuade the girls to come for a walk in the park with me. Natalie was getting her trainers on when Halima came downstairs. She paused and looked Natalie up and down.

'You should not be going out wearing that,' she told her. 'It is not appropriate.'

Natalie looked confused.

'What do you mean?' she asked, puzzled, looking down at the cropped T-shirt and jeans that she was wearing.

'You should be dressing modestly but you can see your flesh,' she said. 'You need to cover up.'

'But my nan bought me this T-shirt,' replied Natalie, looking upset. 'It's my favourite. It's all right isn't it, Maggie?' she asked me. 'Do you think it's OK for me to wear this?'

I was still trying to get my head around what I was hearing.

'Nat, I think what you're wearing is absolutely fine,' I told her. 'I would say if I didn't think it was appropriate.'

Natalie looked up to Halima. She had done her best to be kind and supportive to her and I could see that she was taken aback.

Before we left, I pulled Halima to one side and had a quiet word with her.

'I'm very happy for you to have your own beliefs and wear what you want, lovey,' I told her. 'But I don't think it's fair to impose those beliefs on Nat and criticise her for what she's wearing.'

'It is not right, Maggie,' she replied. 'She should not be dressing like that.'

'Natalie is free to wear whatever she wants, just like you are,' I told her firmly.

Natalie didn't change her T-shirt but I could see that she felt uncomfortable. Just before we left, she ran back upstairs and came back down wearing a hoodie over the top of her T-shirt. I was annoyed with Halima for making her feel self-conscious and question her appearance.

Over the next few weeks, I noticed that Halima's clothing was getting more and more conservative. Whenever she chose things to buy with her allowance, they were always long-sleeved and baggy with high necks. If Natalie and I went into town shopping, she now refused to come with us. When she had first come to live with me, she had loved going shopping with us, but now she would only get clothes from the specialist Islamic shops where she had bought her hijabs.

Soon the girls were off school for half-term and for Natalie it was a chance to plan her Halloween costume. I could see how excited she was.

'Me and Nan used to wait in for the trick or treaters and then try and scare them when they came to the door,' she said.

'I think I'm gonna be a zombie this year,' she said. 'What about you, Halima? What are you going to dress as?'

Halima tutted and shook her head.

'Halloween is a celebration of Satan, who is evil. Everyone should seek refuge in Allah,' she replied coldly.

Natalie's face fell and she looked confused.

'But I love Halloween,' she replied. 'It's fun.'

'We should not celebrate or accept the glorification of evil,' Halima told her firmly.

Her voice had taken on that strange robotic tone again, almost as if she was reading from a script.

'What's she talking about, Maggie?' sighed Natalie. 'I don't understand.'

'Halima, if you don't want to celebrate Halloween, that's absolutely fine and that is your decision,' I told her. 'But I know how much Halloween means to Nat and it's our custom and tradition. Natalie can decide what she chooses to celebrate, just as you can.'

I suggested that Halima could spend the evening upstairs in her bedroom or in the living room so she didn't have to get involved with the trick or treaters who came to the front door.

'But I do not think we should celebrate it at all,' she said, obviously annoyed, and with that, she stormed out of the room. Natalie looked shocked.

'I don't know what's upset her, Maggie, but I love Halloween,' she sighed sadly. 'Nan used to love it too.'

'I know you do, lovey,' I told her. 'You're different people and you both have different belief systems and you have every right to yours as Halima has to hers.'

I went upstairs to see Halima, who was on her laptop. As I walked in, she quickly shut the lid.

'I get that you don't want to celebrate Halloween and that is absolutely fine,' I told her. 'But it's not fair to say that Nat can't celebrate it. It's something she's always done, and for her, it's about having fun. It's a tradition for her and we have to respect that.'

I suggested that if she really wasn't comfortable being here on the thirty-first, then I could talk to Penny and see if there was somewhere else she could go for the evening. But I knew most of my friends and fellow foster carers like Carol and Vicky would be celebrating Halloween with their children too.

'No, it is OK,' she sighed. 'I will stay up here in my bedroom.'

That night I wrote everything down in my notes so I had a record of it. I also talked to Becky about it.

I suppose I was seeking reassurance that I'd done the right thing. I didn't want Halima to feel that I was discriminating against her because of her religion.

'It's not like I'm forcing her to celebrate it or take part,' I told her. 'We're not having a big Halloween party at the house and I'm not dressing up. Natalie will be going to the door to give out sweets to trick or treaters and it will all probably be over by 8.30 p.m. Halima doesn't have to see it or take part in it.'

'Maggie, you don't have to justify yourself,' she said. 'You did the right thing. You're doing your best to meet Halima's cultural and religious needs and that also applies to Natalie too. It's a delicate balancing act.'

'It certainly is.' I smiled. 'Thanks for your support.'

Over the next few days, though, I couldn't shake a niggling feeling that was eating away at me. All these ongoing discussions with Halima about her faith and what being a Muslim meant to her, coupled with the clashes that we were starting to have, had started to make me think. I decided to talk to Penny about my worries when she rang me for a catch-up.

'I feel like the fact that Nat and I aren't Muslim is becoming more and more of an issue for Halima,' I told her. 'Halima and I are having all of these discussions and although I'm more than happy to support her in her faith, I'm starting to have doubts.'

'What kind of doubts?' asked Penny, sounding concerned.

'Doubts about whether I'm the right person to meet her needs,' I sighed.

'Are you saying that you don't want to foster her any more?' asked Penny, her voice tinged with worry. 'Are you giving me notice?'

'Gosh, no, not at all,' I told her. 'I care about Halima an awful lot and I would never do that.'

She had been through so much in her young life and I was desperately trying to give her some stability, love and care.

'It's more about what Halima wants than me,' I continued. 'I just wondered whether she feels that she would be more comfortable living with a Muslim family who know the traditions and customs and live by the Koran too?'

'Let me talk to her,' said Penny.

I knew that, personally, I would be devastated after nearly seven months to see her go but I knew that this wasn't about me and my feelings. My job as a foster carer was to put the child and their interests ahead of mine, so that's what I had to do, no matter how painful it was.

When Penny came round that afternoon, my stomach churned with anxiety about what Halima might say. I watched TV with Nat while they chatted in the kitchen.

Ten minutes later Penny popped her head into the living room and I went out to the hallway to talk to her.

'What did she say?' I asked nervously. 'Does she want to move to another carer?'

She shook her head and relief flooded through my body.

'Not at all.' She smiled. 'She said she's very happy here with you and Natalie. In fact, she looked quite upset when I suggested that she might want to leave,' she added. 'She knows that you're doing your best around her religion, Maggie, and being as inclusive as possible.'

'Good,' I sighed. I was so relieved.

I felt reassured that maybe I *was* handling things OK after all.

The following evening we were due to go to Emaa's house for dinner. She had been so brilliant with Halima and now she invited us round every few weeks. She always kindly invited Natalie too but I tried to time it with the evenings when she was visiting Peggy. I'd come to really enjoy getting to know Emaa, and Halima always seemed so relaxed when we were there. We'd eat delicious Iraqi food and Halima and Emaa would sometimes chat together in Arabic. I knew how important it was for her to maintain some links with her culture.

But when I mentioned it to Halima, she shook her head.

'I don't want to go,' she told me.

I was surprised.

'Why not?' I asked her. 'You love going round there, and I know how much Emaa and the children are looking forward to seeing you.'

Halima looked down at the floor.

'I don't want to see Emaa any more because she has turned her back on Allah, Maggie.'

'What do you mean?' I asked her, taken aback.

'She is not a good Muslim,' she said firmly.

'Halima, you can still be friends with people who don't share the same faith as you,' I told her. 'Natalie and I are not Muslims.'

'But Emaa should be,' she insisted. 'She was born into the faith like me.'

It was clear from her face that she had made her mind up and I couldn't force her to go round there against her will. I was shocked at her sudden change of heart, though, because the pair had developed such a close relationship. It was at Emaa's house that Halima had first talked to us about Iraq and what had happened to her family.

'She's been so supportive to you over the past few months and I know Hattie and William will really miss you,' I told Halima, but she just shrugged.

Despite my worries, I had to keep reminding myself of everything that Halima had been through; all of the trauma and grief that she was still processing and her continual worry and despair about her father and Muhammad. She was also still very isolated and seemed to spend most of her time in her bedroom on the laptop. If her religion was bringing her comfort then that was surely a good thing.

Pull yourself together, Maggie, I told myself firmly.

Even if I didn't entirely understand, I also had to remember that Halima was almost sixteen, and old enough to make some decisions for herself.

She'd started to be more independent now. She got the bus to school and I was pleased when she had asked if she could start getting the bus into the town centre at weekends.

'Of course you can,' I told her, delighted.

I was keen for her to build up her confidence and have some independence. Natalie was eleven and in the first year of secondary school and she was keen to do things on her own too, so one Saturday, I agreed that she could go into town with a friend to look around the shops for a couple of hours.

When she came back, she was full of beans, and couldn't wait to show me the new nail varnish she'd bought with her pocket money.

'Oh, and I saw Halima and her friend when I was out,' she said, as she stood up to take her things upstairs. 'My bus went past them.'

My ears pricked up at the mention of a friend, and I felt a wave of relief.

'Halima didn't say that she was meeting someone,' I said. 'But good for her.'

'I think she was a Muslim too,' Natalie told me.

'Oh, was she wearing a headscarf too?' I asked, interested.

'She was,' said Natalie. 'But hers was black and covered her whole face so there were only her eyes showing.'

'Oh yes, I think they're called niqabs,' I said, remembering my research.

'Is she from your school?'

'I don't think so,' said Natalie. 'I don't think there's anyone at our school who wears a veil like that.'

I was puzzled, but nevertheless, I was thrilled to hear that Halima had made a friend. Maybe this girl was someone from her year who chose to dress more modestly at weekends. When Halima came in, I casually mentioned it to her.

'Nat said she saw you in town today with your friend,' I said. 'How do you know her?'

Halima looked shocked.

'She has no right to say that to you!' she exclaimed. 'Why is she spying on me?'

'She wasn't spying on you,' I told her, surprised by her outburst. 'She was going past on the bus when she saw you, otherwise she would have said hello.

'I'm really pleased that you've got a friend and someone to hang out with,' I went on. 'I was just interested to know more about her. You might even want to invite her round for tea one night.'

But Halima refused to answer. Tears filled her eyes and she stormed off to her room.

I sighed in exasperation. As far as Halima was concerned, I couldn't seem to do anything right at the moment and I was beginning to reach the end of my tether.

THIRTEEN

Secrets

Opening up the laptop, I clicked on the browsing history.

'Maggie, are you sure this is OK?' asked Emaa, looking nervous.

'I've gone around and around in my head about it,' I told her. 'And I've come to the conclusion that this is the only way for me to be sure that Halima is OK.

'If we're being picky about it, it's actually my laptop – I lent it to Halima to do her schoolwork on. I don't want to invade her privacy, but I'm doing it because I'm really concerned about her. I've tried talking to her and got nowhere. I have a duty of care towards her, and right now I feel that I'd be neglecting that if I didn't check in on what she's been looking at online.'

The bottom line was, I was worried. Too many things had been concerning me lately and the only thing I knew for certain was that Halima spent every spare minute that she had on this laptop.

After days spent mulling it over and over in my mind, after the girls had gone to school that morning, I'd fetched my laptop out of her room. But when I'd done a quick check of the websites she had been looking at recently, all of them were in Arabic. I hadn't got a clue what they were or how to begin working it out, so I'd called Emaa and asked her to come round, even though I was going over to her house for a meal that evening. As well as speaking Arabic, Emaa also worked in IT, so she was the perfect person to ask for help.

'Halima's said some things lately that have really started to worry me,' I told her now. 'I know it sounds paranoid, but it just doesn't feel like it's coming from her.'

'In what way?' asked Emaa.

'I don't know,' I sighed. 'There's just something bothering me that I can't put my finger on.'

I had started to worry that, if she'd been trying to trace her father in Iraq or her brother, she may have come across the wrong people or got herself into trouble in some way.

'I can't shake the feeling that she's hiding something from me,' I said.

I was also concerned about the speed at which Halima had suddenly transformed from having little interest in practising her faith to being such a devout Muslim. Some of the language she had been using lately had started to worry me.

'Some of her views just seem very extreme for someone who, a few weeks ago, said she wasn't a practising Muslim,' I sighed. 'And suddenly she doesn't seem to want to mix with people who don't share those views.'

I explained how she was refusing to come to Emaa's house for dinner and was adamant that she didn't want to see her any more.

'Perhaps that was her just being a normal, stroppy teen-ager?' suggested Emaa, who, to my relief, didn't seem in the least bit offended. 'Or she's gone off my cooking?'

'Maybe,' I sighed. 'It seems odd. I just want to be sure that she's OK and not in any trouble.'

I was also annoyed at myself for not putting in more restrictions around the laptop.

'I know hindsight is a wonderful thing, but I really should have policed it more,' I said. 'I was just so pleased she was happy to be using it for her schoolwork and that she seemed so engaged. I naively didn't think to question her much about what she was really doing on it.'

I'd also let her keep the laptop in her room as she needed a quiet place to study.

'You're right, it's probably nothing,' I said. 'You'll probably find it's all harmless teenage stuff and I will have completely wasted your time.'

'Well, let's have a look then and hopefully put your mind at rest,' replied Emaa.

'These are the main Arabic sites that she's been on,' I said, turning the laptop towards her.

'OK,' she said, scanning the screen. 'They look like Muslim chat rooms – places where you can ask questions about the faith.'

She clicked through them on Halima's history, one by one. Eventually she got to an English-speaking chat room.

'Oh wow,' she said suddenly, her brow furrowed. 'This is quite extreme stuff. There's a lot of hatred against the West on this one and talk of "pure Muslims".'

Why on earth would Halima want to be on sites like that? I wondered.

Emaa found that Halima had posted on this particular site three times over the past few months. On the face of it, they seemed very innocuous questions. She was asking about where to buy a hijab and a few other queries about the timing of prayers.

'Hang on,' I said, pointing to the corner of the screen. 'What's that icon there?'

'It's a mailbox where you can send and receive private messages,' Emaa replied, clicking on it.

'Wow, she's been busy,' she gasped.

In Halima's inbox there were hundreds of messages and they were all from the same person – a girl called Zahra.

Zahra had first messaged her after she'd seen her post asking about hijabs.

It's good to see you taking the veil. So many young Muslims don't in the West cos there's so much hate for us.

I felt so sad when I read Halima's reply.

I get called names at school for wearing a headscarf and people refuse to sit with me.

They'd been messaging back and forth for several months. Surprisingly, Halima had told her all about what had happened in Iraq and how she was living in foster care in England and Zahra had replied and told her about her own family. She said she was nineteen and at college.

My parents are originally from Bangladesh, Zahra had written. *I was born in the UK but I hate it here. I feel like I'm trapped between two cultures.*

I felt tears prick my eyes as I read Halima's reply.

I feel very lost and lonely here too, she had written. *I cannot sleep for thinking about my brother and father and wondering where*

*they are. My home is not Iraq any more but it is not here either. I
don't belong anywhere.*

Oh, Halima, I thought. Why didn't you talk to me?

Halima had asked Zahra various questions about Allah and
if Muslims could celebrate Halloween.

*As pure Muslims we should not celebrate or accept the glorifica-
tion of evil,* Zahra had written.

That sounds familiar, I thought, puzzled. Then I suddenly
realised that those were the exact same words that Halima had
said to Natalie. She'd quoted Zahra's response word for word.

'Wow, their messaging has really escalated recently,' said
Emaa.

In the past few weeks Zahra had been contacting Halima
up to twenty times a day.

'Gosh they even arranged to meet up in real life,' gasped
Emaa, who'd read further ahead in the chain of messages.

'What?' I gasped, completely shocked.

*Sister it will be so good to meet you in person at last and talk
about Allah,* Zahra had written.

They'd agreed to meet one Saturday afternoon at the
McDonald's in town.

I was reeling at the fact that unbeknown to me, Halima
had arranged to meet a stranger from the internet and I hadn't
had a clue. My mind went back to the woman Natalie had
seen her with in the niqab. Was this Zahra? From the dates
of the messages, it certainly sounded likely.

But as I read on, it was the messages sent after their meeting
that caused me the most alarm.

*Asalaam Alaikum dear sister, how are you? I hope you are still
interested in taking a holiday as we discussed at our meeting?*

'Taking a holiday?' I questioned, completely puzzled. 'Where on earth would she be going?'

I knew Halima didn't have a passport or indeed any documents.

Emaa clicked down until she got to the most recent messages.

As we spoke about, our brother Abu Rasheed will message you. He saw your photograph and thinks you are very beautiful.

You should see how happy our sisters are in Paradise. They are allowed to be pure Muslims and not sad and lonely like we are here.

'Paradise?' I said aloud. 'And who on earth is Abu Rasheed?'

I had so many questions.

But when I glanced at Emaa, she was sitting with her head in her hands.

'Oh, Maggie, I think I know what's going on here,' she sighed. 'But it can't be true.'

'What?' I asked, totally puzzled by now.

'I think Halima is being recruited.'

'Recruited?' I asked, even more confused. 'For what?'

'IS,' she sighed. 'Or jihadis or terrorists or whatever you want to call them.'

My heart started thumping.

'That's crazy,' I said. 'You've got this all wrong.'

'I might have.' She shrugged. 'It just rings a bell with me.'

She explained how she'd read articles in newspapers about jihadis and the language they used to radicalise people.

'I'm sure "taking a holiday" was a code for going to Syria,' she said. 'And Paradise was what they called it there. They talk in code so they're less likely to be detected online.'

I could feel panic starting to rise up inside me.

'No way, that can't be right,' I said, trying to stay calm. 'Halima has just escaped from a war zone. Why would she go back to one?'

Halima knew the horrors of war first-hand. She'd witnessed terrible things and seen her own mother be killed.

'We need to try and find out who this Abu Rasheed is and if he ever messaged Halima,' said Emaa.

'But how would he contact her?' I asked. 'She doesn't have Facebook and I've already checked her emails and there was nothing on there.'

Emaa started randomly clicking icons on the desktop. She opened file after file but there was nothing except homework documents.

'Ahh yes, this must be it,' she said eventually, opening another app.

'What?' I asked, confused.

'It's an encrypted message app that's hidden behind a calculator icon,' she told me.

I didn't even know what an encrypted message was and felt horribly out of my depth.

'They're secret messages that you can only see if you've got the password – to anyone glancing at them they just look like meaningless random text,' Emaa explained. 'People think they're completely private but there are always ways to read them.'

She clicked and clicked until a screen full of readable messages suddenly appeared. This Abu Rasheed had certainly contacted Halima. There were literally hundreds of messages spanning back over the past few months. I stared at the screen with a mixture of disbelief and horror.

'Oh my God, Emaa, you were right,' I whispered.

All the proof I needed was right in front of me and I felt sick to my stomach.

At first his messages were very flattering and gushing.

Sister Zahra told me about you. She told me you and your family were victims of the West and all of their evils. She sent me your picture and I think you are very beautiful.

He presented himself as a romantic radical fighting the injustices of the West.

What is life like in Raqqa? Halima had asked him.

Life here is good, he wrote. *All pure Muslims have a duty to travel here and help us defend against the threat of the West. Here your sisters have money, they are looked after and have everything they want.*

He'd created this image of a perfect society and a life of opportunity and freedom in an Islamic homeland.

'He's preyed on her vulnerability,' I sighed. 'I bet Zahra told him her story.'

His messages had quickly turned romantic.

I love you more than anything. I will protect and shelter you and keep you safe. You will be treated like a queen in this paradise. Baby no one cares for you like I do. You will be my family.

Halima was definitely more guarded than he was but as his messages had got more lovey-dovey, she had seemed to reciprocate.

I want to be with you too, she had written. *I long to have a family of my own.*

Over time he had bombarded her and twisted her thinking into believing the West was to blame for all of the tragedies she had endured.

It's been hard without my family but I don't mind it in the UK, Halima had told him at one point.

Baby the West is what killed your mother and probably your father and brother. You don't want to live your life with evil Kafirs who hate Muslims when you can be in this paradise with me.

'Kafirs?' I questioned.

Emaa explained that it was a derogatory Arabic term that meant non-believer.

I couldn't believe the sickening things I was reading. He was presenting life in Syria as some sort of dream world where Halima would have money and family.

You will come here and be my wife and I will give you and our children an incredible life while I fight for the Islamic State. It's the only way to be a good Muslim.

In one of his earlier messages, he had sent Halima a photograph of himself. I clicked on it and gasped. He looked as though he was at least in his late twenties and was tall and thin with a long dark beard. He was wearing a Nike tracksuit and was proudly puffing out his chest and clutching a huge gun.

My stomach churned. He was saying that he wanted to marry her and for her to have his children.

'But she's fifteen,' I cried.

This was a grown man. And possibly a violent terrorist at that.

I wasn't angry with Halima; I was just completely devastated that she had felt like this and been so desperate and lost. These people had exploited her vulnerability and capitalised on her grief and loneliness. They were trying to entice her to live in a dangerous war zone and marry a man who was a jihadi.

'I need to call Penny right now,' I said, panicking. 'Then we need to go up to school and get Halima straight away.'

I had absolutely no knowledge or experience of this kind of thing and I felt terrified and completely out of my depth. I was confused, worried and, above all, scared beyond belief for Halima. What on earth had she got herself into?

FOURTEEN

The Painful Truth

My hands were shaking as I picked up the phone and dialled Penny's number.

'Do you want me to leave?' asked Emaa, looking worried.

'No, not at all,' I told her. 'If you don't mind, I'd really appreciate it if you could stay. We might need your help with the computer and, to be honest, I could do with your support,' I added.

'Of course,' she replied, smiling grimly. 'I'll do anything I can to help you and Halima.'

I knew Emaa cared a lot about Halima and I could see that she was completely blindsided by all of this. We both were.

Penny's number rang and rang. My foot jiggled nervously as I willed it not to go to voicemail. It was such a relief when she picked up.

'Hi, Maggie,' she said. 'Is everything OK?'

'Not really,' I told her, trying to keep my voice steady. 'Penny, please could you come round here as soon as you can. I need to talk to you about Halima.'

She could tell by the tone of my voice that it was something serious.

'Of course – I'm due to go into a meeting in a second but I'll make my excuses and leave now,' she told me.

I knew I needed to show her the messages so she could see for herself exactly what had been going on and decide what to do next. I made myself and Emaa a coffee and we both sat at the kitchen table in complete disbelief. I think we were both still in shock at what we'd just discovered. I certainly knew I was struggling to comprehend it. I'd read about jihadi brides, terrorists and radicalisation in newspapers from time to time, but until now, they had just seemed like phrases I'd heard bandied around. I'd never truly believed something like this could happen to normal teenagers in ordinary towns like ours. Never in my worst nightmares could I have imagined that it might happen to a child that I was fostering. I was still reeling from the realisation that all this had been going on under my roof without me having any idea.

Fifteen minutes later, Penny arrived. She'd obviously left in a rush as her usual immaculately coiffed hair was slightly dishevelled and she looked flustered.

'I came as quickly as I could,' she puffed. 'What's going on, Maggie? What on earth has happened?'

I took a deep breath before introducing her to Emaa. Then I explained what we'd found on the laptop that Halima had been using and showed her the messages. Her brow furrowed in concentration as she read through the pages of messages from both Zahra and Abu Rasheed.

'What is all this?' she asked, frowning in confusion.

'We believe that Halima has been radicalised online,' I told her. 'She's been contacted by an Islamic State fighter in Syria who has been trying to entice her to go over there and marry him.'

Penny's mouth gaped open and closed like a goldfish. It was clear she was lost for words.

'But why would Halima want to go and live in Syria?' she gasped. 'She's just escaped from Iraq.'

'My sentiments exactly,' I sighed. 'But you've read this Abu Rasheed's messages. He's basically groomed her and preyed on her. He's painted a picture of this idyllic life where everyone is bound by a common faith and they are all pure Muslims.'

'But how on earth did he get in touch with her in the first place?' asked Penny.

'A young woman contacted her after she posted a few times in a Muslim chat room,' Emaa told her. 'As you can see from her messages, they became friends and she won Halima's trust. They've even met up in town.'

Penny was clearly as taken aback as we were.

'So what should we do now?' I asked, desperate to find some solutions. 'Should we call the police? Do we need to ring the school and bring Halima back here?'

Penny looked stunned and at a loss as to what the next step should be.

'I've heard of these sorts of situations happening, but in all honesty, Maggie, I've never dealt with anything like this myself,' she admitted. 'Let me go and phone my manager. I'll need to liaise with her about what on earth we need to do here.'

She went off into the living room to make some calls. In the meantime, Emaa and I continued to go through the messages and re-read them just in case we had missed something.

My heart ached for Halima. Her loneliness and vulnerability had been exploited as well as her faith. She was already so traumatised and fragile, and I was worried sick about what this was going to do to her. Our main priority was to make sure that she was safe.

It was half an hour before Penny came back into the kitchen.

'I've spoken to my manager and she's as horrified as we are,' she sighed. 'Firstly, she wants me to call the police.'

'Do we have to?' I asked. 'As far as I can see, Halima hasn't committed a crime. She doesn't have a passport to confiscate and we also know that, for now, she's safe at school.'

'I really think we need to log it with them, Maggie,' said Penny and I realised she was right.

Penny's boss knew of a local charity which, as part of their work, helped educate children around the country about radicalisation. They had also helped families of children who had gone to Syria to fight for IS or had been radicalised.

'I've just called Sonia, who runs the organisation,' Penny told us. 'She's very kindly offered to help us with Halima. She's suggested that we collect her from school and bring her to her office and she'll sit with us while we talk to Halima about what has happened and offer us some support and guidance.'

'That's a relief,' I sighed.

Having someone with expertise in a situation like this was sorely needed. We were all out of our depth here and unsure how to handle it properly.

'I'll phone the school now and tell them that we're coming to collect Halima, as we have an urgent appointment,' Penny told me.

'Sonia says the main thing is not to tell Halima that we know what's been going on as she might try and run away before we can get to her, and we don't want to risk that.'

'But what *do* we tell her?' I said, panicking. 'Halima's not stupid. She knows she hasn't got any appointments today and she's going to be suspicious when you and I suddenly turn up and take her out of school.'

'We could tell her that it's a support group for young Muslims and that an appointment came up but you or I forgot to tell her?'

'We can try, I suppose.' I shrugged.

I wasn't sure that she would believe it, but we had to tell her something.

Before we left, I said goodbye to Emaa.

'Thank you so much for everything,' I told her, giving her a hug.

'I'm so sorry this has happened,' she sighed. 'I hope Halima is OK.'

'So do I,' I sighed.

I promised I would call her later and let her know how it had gone. I felt very nervous as we pulled into the school car park and I hesitated before opening the car door.

'We've got to do this, Maggie,' Penny told me firmly. 'We have no other option. We just need to get her to Sonia's office and then we can all talk about this rationally.'

My heart was in my mouth as we walked into the school, and Halima was already sitting in reception waiting for us. She stood up as we walked in.

'Why have you two come here?' she asked, her eyes wide with concern. 'What has happened?'

'Nothing has happened.' Penny smiled.

I could feel my heart pounding as Penny explained that we'd got an appointment with a support group for young Muslims.

'It's a place where you can go to talk about your feelings and there will other Muslim teenagers there,' Penny told her. 'Today we're going to meet the lady who runs it and she's going to tell us about the work they do.'

'But why did you not tell me about this before, Maggie?' Halima asked, looking confused.

'Oh, it's all my silly fault,' I sighed. 'Your name has been on the waiting list for ages and then an appointment came up and I completely forgot to put it on the calendar. It's a good job Penny came to the house today to collect me, otherwise we would have completely missed it.'

Halima nodded slowly, although I wasn't sure that she was convinced.

It suddenly felt very quiet once we were all in the car, and Halima sat in the back seat, not saying a word.

'Why don't I put the radio on?' Penny said, doing her best to act naturally.

We drove for ten minutes to the support group, which was based in an office in the town centre.

'What is the name of this place?' asked Halima as we parked up outside.

Penny hesitated for a moment, before replying, 'Unite.'

I knew both of us were silently praying to ourselves that Halima hadn't heard of it or knew about the work that they did even though that was highly unlikely.

It was only a small office and Sonia was there to meet us. She was in her fifties, with long grey hair and was dressed casually in jeans and a jumper. She had a kind face and seemed very warm and friendly.

Penny introduced us and Sonia shook my hand firmly.

'And you must be Halima.' She smiled. 'Come on in. My colleague Isha's going to take you into our meeting room and get you a drink and a biscuit while I have a quick word with Penny and Maggie.'

Isha was a young woman who was wearing a headscarf and a long black abaya or dress. I could see the fact that she was a Muslim put Halima more at ease.

'We'll see you in a minute,' I told her, trying to reassure her.

Sonia led us into her office. As soon as she closed the door, my body sagged with relief and I flopped down on a chair.

We'd made it and got Halima here safely without her working out what was going on.

'Thank you for helping us out,' Penny told her. 'This has come completely out of the blue for us all and, frankly, we're unsure about how best to proceed.'

'I can completely understand.' Sonia smiled sympathetically. 'I'd like to say it's a rare occurrence but sadly I'm seeing more and more families who are struggling to process what has been happening to their child and they're in shock.'

'I just can't get my head around how this has happened,' I told her, shaking my head. 'How on earth didn't I realise?'

Sonia reassured me that it was a question many parents asked themselves.

'The bottom line is these people are very good at what they do,' she explained. 'They get to know a person and they learn what their weaknesses and insecurities are so that they can play on them.

'You can't blame yourselves,' she continued. 'It's very difficult to spot what's happening. There are very subtle signs and it can also be very quick.

'Some parents literally don't know until their children have left home and are halfway across the world on their way to Syria.'

I shuddered at the thought and felt another wave of relief that we'd found out about Halima in time.

'What I can't get my head around is why would Halima want to go and live in a war zone when she's just escaped from one,' Penny said, looking perplexed. 'She's lived with bombings and shootings and the horror of war. She witnessed her own mother being killed by a car bomb.'

'In my experience it can vary,' answered Sonia. 'Some young women crave the excitement and the danger. They feel empowered by it and it's almost presented to them as a form of feminism. They're sold a vision of a society that needs them in their fight against the West. But from what you've told me, I suspect that's not what happened in Halima's case.'

Sonia explained that other girls, like Halima, were groomed in a similar way to how paedophiles snared their victims.

'They pick on vulnerable young women who they know are alienated and isolated or are having a hard time and they build up their trust and flatter them and say all the right things,' she continued. 'They offer them marriage, promise them the earth and create this vision of a perfect life which couldn't be further from the truth.'

'It's just horrendous,' I sighed.

This man had offered Halima exactly what she wanted: a sense of belonging and a community where everyone was the same and looked out for each other.

Sadly, what Sonia was saying made sense. Despite all our efforts, it was obvious from her messages that Halima had felt incredibly lonely and alienated. She had a deep yearning to belong and have a family of her own as hers had been destroyed, and Abu Rasheed had offered her that.

I was only grateful for one thing.

'I'm so relieved that we found all of this out now and not after she had gone,' I sighed.

At least we could stop it from happening.

'But how would she have even got over to Syria?' asked Penny. 'She doesn't have a passport or any documents.'

'These things can all be faked or falsified,' replied Sonia. 'Her recruiter would have organised it all for her and given her instructions about what to do and when to travel. It sounds highly likely that this young woman who befriended her in the chat room was a recruiter who offered her friendship and won her trust and then put her in touch with Abu Rasheed.'

Sonia described how the usual route was a flight to Turkey then a long, difficult and dangerous journey across the border into Syria and then into IS territory.

It was terrifying hearing all of this and knowing how close Halima had come to choosing this life for herself, leaving the country and putting herself in grave danger.

'Do you know if they are already married?' asked Sonia.

Penny and I looked at each other, confused.

'Well, no, of course not – Halima's still here,' I told her.

'Unfortunately, they don't need to be in Syria to get married,' Sonia explained. 'There have been cases where IS fighters have married young women and leaders officiate the ceremony online.'

Penny and I looked at each other in horror.

'There was nothing in any of the encrypted messages that suggested a marriage had already taken place,' I told her. 'He spoke about Halima becoming his wife but that was all.'

'Good.' Sonia nodded. 'But I do think it's something that we need to ask Halima.'

There was something else that I'd been thinking about throughout all of this. Something that had been niggling away at me.

'Do you really think Halima would have actually gone through with it?' I asked Sonia. 'Or do you think all of this is just a game or a teenage fantasy?'

I knew that for teenagers, the online world was more like a fantasy world and not a real one.

'It's hard to know.' Sonia shrugged. 'It could have been a form of escapism for Halima but equally it could be real and something that she was days or weeks away from intending to do.

'I definitely think it's dangerous to treat it as some impossibility that would never really happen because many young girls from around the world do make the journey to Syria and they never come home again.'

We had to treat this as a real threat.

Then came the moment that I'd been dreading.

'We'd better go and talk to Halima,' sighed Penny.

'I think it's best if you do the talking and explain to Halima what you've found out, but if it's OK with you, I'll sit with you and I can offer any help or support where needed,' suggested Sonia.

'That would be brilliant, thank you,' Penny said gratefully.

As we walked out of the office, I could see Halima sitting in the meeting room chatting to Isha. As soon as the three of us walked in, she looked up at us with her big dark eyes and I could see they were filled with fear.

She knows what's coming, I told myself.

I sat next to Halima while Penny and Sonia sat at the other side of the table facing her.

'Halima, we need to talk to you about something very serious. This morning Maggie found some things on your computer that were extremely concerning,' Penny began.

Halima looked terrified.

'But that's my computer and it is private,' she exclaimed, her eyes wide.

Penny ignored her protests and went on.

'Halima, we found some messages that suggest you've been communicating with a man in Syria,' she told her. 'We believe that he is an IS fighter and that you were intending to travel over there and get married to him.'

Tears filled Halima's eyes.

'Why are you saying all these things?' she sighed, shaking her head. 'It is not true.'

'Halima, lovey, we saw all the messages on the laptop,' I told her. 'We know that Zahra contacted you in a chat room and that you've been talking to her over the last few months.'

'Zahra is my friend!' Halima cried. 'Am I not allowed to have a friend?'

'Halima, we also saw the messages from Abu Rasheed,' Penny told her.

'You had no right!' she yelled, anger rising. 'Those messages were private. You should not have been able to read them.'

I tried to put my arm around her, but she shrugged me off as she wept silently.

'Halima, you're not in any trouble,' I reassured her. 'You're the victim here. We know how much you've been through and how much sadness you've had in your life. This man has taken advantage of that. But we need you to be honest with us and tell us the truth.'

Penny gently explained that we thought Zahra and Abu Rasheed had radicalised and groomed her.

'No, they have not!' snapped Halima. 'They are the only ones who understand me and my culture. Abu Rasheed was going to look after me and keep me safe.'

He'd made himself out to be her strong, protective knight in shining armour who was going to rescue her from the evil West.

'Halima, he has preyed on the fact that you are young and vulnerable,' I told her, but she shook her head, sobbing into her hands.

Penny and I looked at each other. We were at a loss to make her understand so I think we were both relieved when Sonia stepped in to help.

'Halima, Abu Rasheed was trying to get you to join a terror group,' Sonia told her seriously. 'A terror group that is responsible for brutal violence and many, many deaths.'

'The West are the terrorists,' said Halima. 'IS is a state that all Muslims must join. It is our duty.'

She was speaking in that same robotic voice again. It was truly terrifying to see how she had become so indoctrinated.

Sonia was very calm and measured as she continued.

'Halima, the fact is Syria is a war zone just like Iraq was,' she told her. 'You know more than any of us what it's like to live in a war zone. There are bombs falling and air strikes and shootings.

'Abu Rasheed has promised you this perfect life with everything you could ever want, but the reality is that many women and girls who go out there find themselves living in horrific, cramped conditions. They get there and they realise this life is very, very different to the one that they were promised.

'There isn't proper housing, electricity or running water. Many of them get sick, along with their children, and sometimes they die.'

Halima started to cry.

'Why don't they come back then?' she sobbed.

'Many of them want to but they can't,' sighed Sonia. 'The reality is, once you're there it's very difficult to get out. Many don't make it out alive.

'Many girls like you go over there and they are frightened and more alone than ever, but there is no going back. Some of them have been killed in air strikes, some are killed because they're trying to escape. Even those who manage to escape often aren't allowed back to their home countries. They quickly become disillusioned and realise it's not the utopia these people have made it out to be.

'They have been tricked. You are promised heaven but in reality it's hell.'

It was harsh, but Halima needed to hear these words. She needed to know the truth.

'You are telling lies to me,' she said angrily. 'You are trying to put me off. How do you know what life is like there? You are not a Muslim.'

Sonia's eyes filled with tears and she took Halima's hand.

'I know because my own son was radicalised too. He left his home and his family and he went to Syria, and that's where he died.'

Halima's face fell.

'I am so sorry,' she whispered, and dissolved into tears.

I put my arms around her and hugged her as she cried. I had no idea how she was ever going to get over this.

FIFTEEN

The Aftermath

Halima was transfixed as Sonia started to tell us about her nineteen-year-old son Ben. She explained how he was studying engineering at university.

'Our family weren't religious but some of his mates at uni were Muslims and in his second year, he converted to Islam,' she said. 'We were surprised, but we were happy to support him in his new faith.'

Sonia went on to describe how, in a matter of months, Ben had started to change.

'My happy-go-lucky, chatty son withdrew into a quiet shell of a boy,' she sighed. 'I tried to talk to him, to reach out to him, but he pushed me away.'

Several months later, Ben left for university one morning and never came home. Sonia described how, as the days went by, they frantically rang around his friends and called the police, but no one could tell them where Ben was. They discovered that, before he left, he'd destroyed the hard drive of his computer. Three weeks later, they got a brief text from

Ben saying he had gone to Syria to join IS and had been sent to a camp for military training. He said he wasn't allowed to contact them again. It was the last time Sonia would ever hear from her son.

'Five months later, I received a call from another IS fighter congratulating me on the fact that my only son was now a martyr,' said Sonia, her voice choking up with emotion. 'He'd died in a drone strike five months after flying out to Syria.'

'I'm so sorry,' I whispered, tears stinging my eyes.

Halima looked distraught.

'When I lost my son, I knew my life would never be the same again,' sighed Sonia, wiping her eyes. 'My heart will always be broken, but I vowed that if I could help other parents to spot the signs before it's too late, then Ben's death wouldn't be in vain.'

It had been this desire to help that had led her to start up her organisation.

'Halima, we're here to help you,' Sonia went on. 'I know how convincing these people can be. All we want to do is keep you safe, and believe me, Syria is not safe.'

Halima looked stunned, but she nodded slowly.

'Thank you so much for helping us today,' Penny said as we got up to leave.

'I'll be in touch to organise some follow-up sessions for Halima,' she said.

I couldn't stop myself from giving her a hug as we walked out.

'I'm so sorry about your son, Sonia,' I told her. 'I can't even begin to imagine what you've been through.'

Penny drove us back to the house in silence. Halima looked dazed as she stared out of the window, and she didn't say a word. My heart broke for her and I wondered what was going on in her head. She'd been through such a lot. How much trauma could one young girl take?

When we got home, she went straight up to her room without saying a word.

'What on earth do we do now?' I sighed to Penny. 'How the hell do I help her move forwards from this?'

'We'll work it out,' she replied. 'When things have calmed down a little, Sonia's offered to do some one-to-one sessions with her and help her try to make sense of what's happened.'

Sonia had explained to us that she ran a de-radicalisation programme that was designed to help young people see why the beliefs that they held were wrong.

Our immediate priority was to put a plan in place to make sure that Halima was safe.

'Maggie, I'd like you to drive her to school like you did in the early days rather than her go on the bus,' asked Penny. 'Can you also speak to the school and make sure they know that she's not to be let out until you collect her from reception?'

I agreed to go up to the school the following morning and tell them what had happened.

'Are you happy for me to share the whole story with them? I'd imagine they're going to want to know why I'm suddenly putting in all these restrictions.'

'Absolutely.' Penny nodded. 'They need to know exactly what's going on so they can keep an eye out for anything suspicious. We all need to be aware of what's happened and work together on this.'

We didn't truly know how radicalised Halima had become and we couldn't take the risk of her suddenly trying to communicate with Abu Rasheed again or disappearing off to Syria. It was unthinkable and I knew that I'd never forgive myself.

Penny had to leave as she had an appointment at the police station to discuss Halima's case. She'd called them earlier that day and they'd asked her to bring the laptop in.

'I'm going to tell them what's happened and give them the laptop so they can download the messages,' she said. 'They might want to speak to Halima too.'

As far as I could see, Halima hadn't broken the law. She hadn't openly expressed extremist views in her messages or talked about planning acts of terrorism, and nor had Zahra. Both Zahra and Abu Rasheed had cleverly used code whenever they were talking about Halima going to Syria. There was nothing that incriminated either of them, but the police still needed to know about it.

'Let's keep in touch, Maggie, and ring me straight away if you have any concerns,' Penny told me.

'I will.' I nodded.

After Penny had gone, I went up to check on Halima in her bedroom. She was lying on the bed and I could tell she had been crying.

'Are you angry with me, Maggie?' she asked quietly, as I sat down beside her.

'Not at all,' I told her, meaning it. 'I feel very sad and worried about what has happened to you. You are the victim here. You've been taken advantage of and that's a horrible thing to happen. We're all here for you and our main aim now is to keep you safe.'

I explained that a few things would need to happen in order for us to do that.

'I'm afraid you won't have access to the laptop or the internet any more,' I told her. 'If you need the internet for your homework then you can use my tablet, but it will always be downstairs and I'll need to sit with you while you're using it.

'And it will only be websites in English,' I added.

Halima nodded.

I also explained that I would be taking and collecting her from school again.

'But you are treating me like I am a little baby,' she sighed. 'You do not trust me any more.'

'At this moment in time, it's not about trusting you, it's about keeping you safe,' I told her firmly. 'My job is to protect you. That's what foster carers do, we protect the children that we're looking after. You have to understand that this is very serious, Halima.'

'What happens if Abu Rasheed tries to contact me and I don't respond?' she asked in a small voice. 'What if he gets angry if I do not reply to his messages?'

'Then he will have to get angry,' I told her. 'The police will close down the messaging app and your email account so Abu Rasheed will soon realise that you don't want to be in contact with him any more and that you are not going to be travelling to Syria.'

'What about Zahra?' she asked.

'The same thing will happen with Zahra,' I replied. 'If she messages you via the chat room, her messages will bounce back and she'll realise your account isn't active any more.'

'But she was my friend,' sighed Halima.

'She was a recruiter, Halima,' I told her firmly. 'Her job was to befriend vulnerable girls like you, plant the seed, work out your weaknesses and then introduce you to Abu Rasheed.'

It was harsh for Halima to hear, but I knew it was important for her to know the truth.

Eventually, I persuaded her to come downstairs, just as Natalie was walking through the door.

'How come you're home already, Halima?' she asked. 'Why weren't you at school this afternoon?'

'Oh, we had a meeting with her social worker,' I told her casually.

However, Natalie could tell there was something wrong.

'Are you OK, Halima?' she asked her. 'You look sad. Have you been crying?'

Halima didn't say a word. She turned around and bolted back upstairs.

'I didn't mean to upset her,' Natalie grumbled. 'She's been acting so weird lately.'

I took Natalie into the kitchen.

'Halima's had a very hard day today, flower,' I told her. 'Penny and I have had a few concerns about her safety so there are a couple of things I need to talk to you about.'

I explained that I'd be driving Halima to school like I used to and picking her up from the office.

'So that means I can give you a lift too,' I told her.

'No way,' said Natalie, grimacing. 'That's way too embarrassing. I want to get the bus with my mates.'

I also explained that Halima wasn't allowed access to the internet or a laptop without my permission.

'So under no circumstances are you to lend her your phone or let her go on the computer,' I told her.

165

'OK.' She nodded. 'But why, Maggie?'

'I'm afraid that's confidential information and it's not fair on Halima if I disclose it to you,' I replied.

'Aw, nobody ever tells me anything,' she sighed and she stormed off to her room too.

In a way, I was glad of the peace. I made myself a cup of tea and sat down at the kitchen table. This was the first time that I'd had to stop for a moment and try to process what had gone on that day. It had all happened so fast. I was still reeling from the fact that I'd had absolutely no idea this had been going on under my roof. It was terrifying how someone could have manipulated Halima so quickly and convincingly to the point where she was prepared to leave the country and travel to a war zone. But my overriding emotion was still one of sheer relief that we had found out and stopped it before it had got to that point. These people had completely tapped into her vulnerability and lack of self-confidence and I knew now that this was no teenage fantasy. Halima had had every intention of one day getting on that plane, if she could. It was clear that she was very confused about who she was and where she belonged.

I was still lost in my own thoughts when Penny called from the police station.

'Maggie, I've just finished talking to the police. It's urgent that we find out whether Halima told Zahra your address or the name of her school. The same with Abu Rasheed. Did she ever give either of them those details or speak to them on the phone?'

I felt sick. In my panic, I hadn't even thought of those things.

I quickly ran upstairs to check with Halima. She looked terrified as I repeated the questions Penny had asked, but to my relief, she promised me that she hadn't told them any details that meant they could find her here.

'No, I think we're OK,' I told Penny, relief flooding through me. 'Zahra knew that she lived somewhere near town but Halima never told her the name of her school or gave her this address. She says she only ever corresponded with Abu Rasheed via encrypted messages and nothing else.'

Halima had continually been asking me for a mobile and I'd been looking into getting her one, but I was so relieved now that I hadn't bought one as it would have been another means of communication and another way for them to access her.

Despite everything that had gone on in the last twenty-four hours, I knew it was vital that life carried on as normal; for Halima's sake as much as anything else.

'Does my school know?' Halima asked me anxiously the next morning as she got ready.

'I'm going to talk to them about it now,' I told her.

After I'd walked her into the building, I went to see Ms Hicks in her office. She was shocked when I went through what had been happening.

'We don't have any experience of dealing with this kind of thing,' said Ms Hicks. 'As you know, we're not a hugely multi-cultural school and Halima is one of only three Muslim pupils.'

'There can be many types of extremism, and it isn't neces-sarily about someone being a Muslim,' I told her. 'It can be someone who later converts or doesn't seem outwardly religious. Every young person, no matter what their religious beliefs, is at risk.'

After talking to Sonia, I had started to realise that radicalisation was an issue that was becoming an increasing problem in our society, and one that everyone needed to be more aware of.

Penny had already emailed Ms Hicks about the urgent strategy meeting that was being held at Social Services the following day and she was going to attend it.

'What do we need to do in the short term?' asked Ms Hicks.

'Just keep an eye on Halima,' I told her. 'Look out for anything suspicious but also just check that she's OK. It's been a very emotional twenty-four hours for her.'

'Do you think she might try and get in touch with these people again?' Ms Hicks asked.

'On the face of it, she seems devastated and shocked to learn the truth about their intentions, and I hope that she fully understands the danger she was in, but I think it's naive to assume anything any more.'

After everything that had happened, I knew I was going to be watching Halima like a hawk.

The following day, it was the emergency strategy meeting at Social Services. The room was packed. There was Becky and Penny, Ms Hicks, Halima's IRO Lydia and a police officer. Sonia had come along too.

'We've called this meeting after the events that happened a couple of days ago,' began Lydia after she'd introduced everyone. 'At this stage, Halima's safety is our number one priority and we need to weigh up the risks.'

She explained that this issue was a relatively new one for the local authority.

'Social Services, including most of us present, have never had to deal with a radicalisation case like this before, so we are all learning,' she told us.

The police officer, a softly spoken man in his thirties, explained that they had downloaded the messages from my laptop.

'We have logged it all with the Counter Terrorism Unit to see if they are individuals known to them or are linked into any other case,' he said. 'Even if we were able to trace Zahra through the IP address of her computer, it seems unlikely that there are any charges we can bring against her as she was very careful about what she said.'

I explained that Halima no longer had access to the internet and didn't have a mobile phone, as well as the fact that I would be taking her to and from school for the foreseeable future.

'This is such a unique situation for Social Services but it's something that we need to learn from so that, going forward, we have set procedures in place on how to deal with it,' said Lydia. 'I think it's also important that we start to offer specific training for carers about how to recognise the signs.'

I nodded.

'It was certainly something that I didn't know to look out for,' I added.

Sonia also gave us her input.

'I do know that in these situations, it has to be a united effort, with people from all areas of a child's life working together.'

It was clear that school would have a big part to play in all this.

'Our focus needs to be on making Halima feel less alienated, and try to integrate her more into the school community,' agreed Ms Hicks. 'We're currently looking at how we can do that.'

'What's her relationship like with her teachers?' asked Lydia.

'She has a strong bond with her art teacher, Miss Morgan, that we've talked about before,' replied Ms Hicks.

'Oh yes,' remembered Lydia. 'Halima goes to her art room at break time. Could she perhaps set up a small club at lunchtime or after school for pupils that enjoy art so that Halima could start to make friends with some of her peers?'

'It's certainly something we can talk to Miss Morgan about,' agreed Ms Hicks. 'What's happened has also made us look into the whole issue of integration and how we can do better on that front in the future.'

Although I felt overwhelmed by everything that had happened, it was also reassuring for me to hear that other people hadn't been aware of this type of issue before now either. It was the unknown for all of us.

'All we can do is be aware and keep talking to each other about things,' concluded Lydia. 'If something doesn't feel right, no matter how small, please talk to Penny.'

I'd just got home from the meeting when there was a knock at the front door. I opened it to see my friend Vicky standing there. I don't know whether it was her catching me unawares or just the joy of seeing a friendly face after such an intense couple of days, but when I opened the door and saw her, I burst into tears.

'Maggie,' she said, concerned. 'What is it? What on earth's happened?'

We went through to the kitchen and she made me a coffee while I dried my eyes and tried to compose myself.

As Vicky was also a foster carer as well as a trusted friend, I could talk to her about what had happened with Halima. As I explained what had gone on, she was horrified.

'How frightening,' she gasped. 'I've read about girls being radicalised and going abroad but I never thought it could really happen here, or to girls like Halima, if you know what I mean,' she said, and I nodded.

'Me neither,' I replied.

Vicky let me talk freely, and all my worries poured out.

'I think I handled it all wrong,' I sighed. 'Why didn't I keep tighter controls on the laptop? Why didn't I spot the signs?'

'Maggie, it's OK,' she soothed. 'You have to know that you're not to blame. You did your best and you have stopped it now, before anything really bad happened.'

'But have we stopped it?' I sobbed. 'Have we really?'

In all honesty, I didn't know. All I could think about when I closed my eyes at night was Sonia's face and her despair as she described how she had watched her son walk out of the front door that morning to go to university. One normal day, nothing out of the ordinary, and she had never seen him again.

Had Halima really told us everything? Were there other people that she was talking to about going to Syria? I'd read somewhere that girls tended to travel in groups. Were there friends we didn't know about or pupils at her school? Could we and should we trust her? Or was there a chance that she might walk out of my house one morning and never come back?

My head was just full of these questions, going round and round in my mind.

I had never dealt with anything like this in the entirety of my fostering career and I just didn't know any more. It had rocked me to the core and I was starting to question everything.

SIXTEEN

Questions

A young woman in a black hijab talked into the camera, her blue eyes filled with fear and her cheeks streaked with tears.

'My baby died because there were no doctors or medicine,' she wept. 'I'm so scared of my other children getting sick, and we don't have enough food or clean water.

'Every day I'm angry,' she sighed. 'I'm angry with myself. I'm angry that no one told me this is what life would be like here.

'Every day I ask myself why I left my home and my family to come to this hell. But it doesn't matter, because now I'm trapped, and I can't leave.'

Poor, poor woman.

I swallowed the lump in my throat and wiped away a tear.

I looked at Halima who was sitting beside me, staring intently at the grainy footage on the screen.

She had started coming to the centre twice a week for one-to-one sessions with Sonia. Tonight, we were watching a short film about three young women who had left their homes in France to travel to Syria. Sonia had invited me to come along as she thought it would be useful for me to see it too. It wasn't an easy watch. The women described how they were treated as domestic slaves, how they were raped by their husbands and passed around to other IS fighters. They talked about children being given guns or threatened with being forced to be suicide bombers, and babies dying because they were dehydrated and malnourished.

It was utterly heartbreaking and brutal, and I shuddered at the thought of Halima ending up in a place like that.

When the film was over, Sonia turned the lights on and came and sat with us.

'What did you think of that, Maggie?' she asked.

'It was so harrowing,' I sighed. 'I can't imagine living in such fear every day and not being able to escape.'

'What about you, Halima?'

Halima looked bewildered.

'I feel very sad for them all,' she replied.

It was a tough lesson, but I could see that Sonia was trying to show her the reality of this perfect society that she had been promised.

I was glad that Sonia had invited me along so that I could watch the film too. It meant that Halima could talk to me about it later if she wanted to. When we got home, we had dinner with Natalie. Halima didn't say much, and I could see that she was exhausted.

That night, as I lay in bed, all I could think about was the young woman in the film whose baby had died. There was something about her eyes that haunted me – an utter blank-ness about them as if she had given up on life.

I was willing myself to sleep when a scream suddenly echoed through the house. I was now used to Halima's screams, but this was unlike any noise that I'd heard her make before – it was raw and primal.

I ran down the landing to her bedroom. She was lying on her side, her legs pressed up to her chest, rocking backwards and forwards. Her hair was damp with sweat and she was screaming and screaming.

'Ana asif Mama,' she wept in Arabic. 'Ana asif.'

I gently shook her awake and her eyes snapped open.

Confused, she looked around the room.

'Hal faealt dhlk?' she asked.

'I don't understand Arabic, lovey, you need to talk in English,' I reminded her.

'Did I do it, Maggie?' she asked me, her eyes wide.

'Did you do what?'

'Did I kill Mama?'

With that, she burst into tears again. I held her trembling body in my arms.

'You've had a horrible nightmare, flower,' I soothed. 'You didn't kill your mum, Halima. Remember she died when a car bomb exploded?'

I could see how frightened she was.

'My nightmare was about him,' she whimpered.

By 'him' I knew instantly that she meant Abu Rasheed.

'He forced me to plant the bomb in the car. He made me kill my own mother and watch her be blown up. I can feel my ears ringing again like they did that day and the car alarms going off. I feel like I'm going mad.'

She buried her head into my shoulder and sobbed.

'Oh, Halima,' I sighed. 'I'm so sorry. It's just a nightmare. None of that is true and Abu Rasheed can't hurt you any more.'

Everything that had happened in the past few weeks was becoming jumbled in her head with the trauma she had experienced in Iraq. She was so vulnerable, but I knew that all I could do was keep reassuring her and repeating the same things to her.

'Remember you are not to blame for any of this,' I told her. 'You are the victim.'

'But what if I had gone to Syria to marry him?' she asked. 'What would have happened to me? Would I have been like the women in that film?'

'I don't know, lovey, but thankfully you didn't go and that's the important thing,' I told her firmly. 'You are safe here and there are lots of people who care about you and want to support you.'

After what had happened, she was starting to question everything.

One morning Halima came down for breakfast and I noticed that she wasn't wearing her hijab.

'Oh, are you not putting your headscarf on today?' I asked her casually.

'No,' she replied, looking at the floor. 'I don't think I can be a Muslim any more. All of this happened because I was a Muslim.'

The poor girl was so confused.

'This didn't happen because of your faith, Halima,' I told her. 'This happened because people took advantage of your vulnerability. You were being groomed and that happens to non-Muslims too. It's about people imposing their beliefs on you, trying to control and manipulate you.'

I talked to Sonia about it when I dropped her off for her next session.

'I'll get Isha to talk to her about it,' she said. 'They can look at the Koran together and talk about what it means to be a Muslim and how it's about peace, and nothing to do with violent extremism.'

Halima's school was also doing its best to try and integrate her more. Miss Morgan had been brilliant and had started a lunchtime art club that Halima attended twice a week with seven other students. Each week they had a task connected to a different theme and she seemed to be really enjoying the sessions. She always brought home her creations and we would look at them together.

One week the theme was language and she showed me a small clay vase that she'd painted Arabic text onto.

'It's really beautiful and so delicate.' I smiled.

'You can have it if you want,' she told me shyly, and I gave it pride of place on the shelves in the living room.

We talked about what it had been like to use clay as it was something that Halima hadn't done before.

'Poppy is very good with clay,' she said. 'She has made things with clay on a special wheel that spins round very fast.'

'Oh, you mean a potter's wheel.' I nodded. 'I've always wanted to have a go on one of those.'

I'd noticed that the name Poppy had cropped up a few times in our conversations recently. Halima told me she went to art club and was in her year but a different tutor group. I didn't ask lots of questions or draw attention to it but I was hopeful that a friendship was blossoming. It was much easier now Halima's spoken English was so good.

'You can invite Poppy round for tea one night if you want?'
I told her.

'Yes, I would like that,' said Halima. 'I will ask her
tomorrow.'

One week, the theme of art club was 'home' and Halima
had done some drawings that she was keen to show me. We
sat down at the kitchen table and she got them out of her bag.
She'd done a series of pencil sketches all about life in Iraq.

'What's this one about?' I asked her.

'It's my mother's hands at the sink scooping the seeds out
of a pomegranate,' she said.

She talked me through each one. They were simple but
beautifully done. Another one was a sketch of the yard at the
back of their house in Baghdad.

'That's Muhammad's football on the ground.' Halima
smiled. 'He was always kicking it around. And Mama's abayas
and scarfs drying in the sun.'

She smiled sadly. Her third sketch was of a pair of shoes.

'Whose are those?' I asked.

'My father's,' she replied. 'As a Muslim, you are not allowed
to wear shoes in the house, so he always used to leave his by
the front door. That's the last thing I remember about home.
As Muhammad and I left that night, all I can remember is
seeing his shoes by the door . . . That feels like a very long
time ago,' she sighed.

'It was,' I told her, giving her hand a reassuring squeeze.

Although I could see that these memories had upset her,
I was struck by how much her artwork had changed in the
eight months that she had been with me. I remembered the
drawings and paintings that Miss Morgan had showed me

when Halima had first started at school. I'd never forget the contorted faces and the barbed wire, the blood and pile of dead bodies. Everything had been about death, pain, bloodshed and violence. Halima had been through so much recently and I knew from her nightmares that the trauma was still there, but these pictures were softer somehow. They were still powerful, but they were beautiful too. In each one I could still feel her sense of loss and longing for her family but there was a calmness and a peace about them.

With everything that had been going on with Halima, I was also worried about Louisa too. One morning she rang and asked if she could come round.

'Of course you can, lovey,' I told her. 'You know you're welcome anytime.'

This was progress as, in the two months since Dominic had died, she had hardly left the house, and I had always gone to visit her.

'You look a bit chirpier,' I told her as she came in.

She still looked tired, but she'd had her hair cut and was wearing make-up. It was a relief to see her looking more like her old self again.

'I'm trying to get out a bit more,' she told me. 'And last week I started counselling.'

'Good for you, flower,' I said. 'I really hope that it helps to talk to someone.'

'So, what's been going on with you, Maggie?' she asked, sipping her tea. 'I feel really out of the loop with you and the girls.'

'Oh, nothing much,' I told her. 'We're all OK.'

I couldn't tell her what had been happening with Halima for confidentiality reasons. If Louisa was still living with me then that would be a different matter but I didn't want to burden her with my problems either.

'Maggie, there's something I wanted to chat to you about,' she told me. 'I've decided to go back to work. Charlie thinks it's too soon but I'm going mad moping round the flat. What do you think?'

'I think you have to do what feels right for you,' I told her. 'If you feel ready then do it.'

'I do.' She nodded. 'I know I'll be around lots of babies and toddlers, but I have to get used to it. I can't just stay in the flat for the rest of my life.'

'I'm so proud of you,' I told her, giving her a hug.

Every day I thought about her and my loft full of baby things and I wished with all my heart that things had turned out differently.

A few weeks later it was Halima's sixteenth birthday.

'I don't really feel like doing anything,' she sighed.

'We should mark it,' I told her. 'After everything that has happened, you deserve a celebration.'

Unbeknown to Halima, I arranged for us all to go over to Emaa's house. I'd made a birthday cake and bought her a silver bracelet with a little heart pendant on it from me and Natalie. I knew it was going to be a hard day for her as these special occasions always brought up memories of family and the past.

It was the first time Halima had seen Emaa for weeks, and Hattie and William leapt into her arms. I'd kept in touch with

Emaa and let her know what had been going on since we found the messages on the computer.

I could see Halima was embarrassed.

'I'm sorry I have not seen you for a while,' Halima told her. 'I've been figuring a few things out.'

'That's OK.' Emaa smiled. 'The past is in the past. Today it's all about celebrating you.'

'Thank you.' She smiled bashfully.

Emaa had gone to so much trouble and there was a huge table covered in lots of different Iraqi dishes for us all to try.

We had a lovely evening of food, chatter and laughter. It wasn't until I was leaving that I looked at my phone that had been in my handbag hanging by Emaa's front door.

I was worried when I saw I had four missed calls from Penny and finally a voicemail.

When I listened to it, she sounded frantic.

'Maggie, please can you call me back urgently,' she said. 'I've just had a call from the charity that were trying to trace Halima's family. They've got some news about her brother.'

My heart sank. Suddenly the happy evening we'd just had was well and truly over.

SEVENTEEN

Lost and Found

My heart pounded in my chest as Penny explained that she'd had a call from the charity that Halima had had the appointment with several weeks ago.

I prepared myself for bad news and my hands were shaking as I held the phone to my ear.

'Maggie, her brother's alive!' Penny told me. 'And they've got a possible address for him.'

'What?' I gasped. 'That's amazing!'

Although I would never had said it to Halima, when she'd told us what had happened in the sinking dinghy that night at sea, I hadn't held out much hope that Muhammad had survived.

I had so many questions.

'Where is he?' I asked. 'Can she see him?'

I expected Penny to say Greece or Turkey or even perhaps that he had gone back to Iraq. So when Penny said the name of a city two hours away from me, I nearly dropped my mobile in shock.

'All this time and he's been in the UK too?' I gasped.

'I don't know how long he's been here,' replied Penny. 'All I know is that the name Muhammad Hussein came up in a Social Security search and the date of birth is the same. Obviously at this point we can't be 100 per cent sure that it's him, as it's a fairly common name.'

'So what happens now?' I asked.

Penny had written a letter that the charity would forward on to the address, explaining the situation and asking Muhammad to get in contact if he wanted to get in touch with his sister.

'I put my phone number on it,' added Penny. 'And I also said to please let us know if this wasn't the right person.'

I was still reeling with shock.

'Obviously we can't say a word to Halima at this point,' Penny told me. 'I don't want to get her hopes up. It might not be the right Muhammad, and even if it is, he might not want to have contact with her.'

I desperately hoped that it was Halima's brother and if it was, I was sure that he would want to see her. It was so hard not saying anything to Halima and I was impatient for news.

I didn't have to wait very long. Penny called the following day.

'It's him,' she told me. 'Muhammad has just rung me. He called as soon as he opened the letter.

'Oh, Maggie, he was so emotional, he was crying down the phone,' she added. 'He's desperate to see Halima.'

'I'm so, so pleased.' I smiled.

Penny had arranged to go and see him the following day. It was important for her to meet him in person and check everything seemed OK with him before we reunited him with Halima. It had been over a year since she'd last seen him and Social Services needed to make sure there were no obvious issues or addiction problems before we put her back in touch with her brother.

'I'm sure he's going to have lots of questions about Halima so I wondered if you would be able to come with me, Maggie?' Penny asked.

'Of course, I'd be happy to,' I told her. 'I'd love to meet him.'

We could get there and back in enough time while Halima was at school. As I watched her eat her breakfast the following morning, I was bursting with excitement.

If only she knew where I was going today, I thought to myself.

As soon as I'd dropped her off at school, Penny was waiting at my house to pick me up and we drove to the city where Muhammad was living. He had a ground-floor flat in a small block close to the city centre.

'What does he do for work?' I asked her.

'He's just started a job in a haulage warehouse,' Penny told me.

We knocked on the door and a young man came to answer it. He was tall, well over six foot, and very thin. He had short black hair, dark brown eyes just like Halima's and the same prominent nose. He was wearing jeans and a T-shirt.

'Hi, are you Muhammad Hussein?' asked Penny and he nodded.

'I'm Penny, your sister's social worker, and this is Maggie, her foster carer.'

'Thank you for coming here,' he said, giving us a little bow. Please,' he said, gesturing for us to come in.

The flat was small, and the mismatched furniture looked like it had been cobbled together from charity shops, but although it was basic, it was clean and tidy.

'How long have you been here?' I asked him.

'Two months,' he replied. 'I was in a hostel before this.'

'Your English is very good,' Penny commented, and he nodded, looking pleased.

'I try.' He shrugged. 'You pick up quick. And Halima?' he asked.

'She has good English now too,' I told him. 'She learnt very quickly at school.'

He made us a cup of tea and then he explained how he had got to the UK.

'The boat, it was sinking,' he said. 'I was very frightened and I was shouting for Halima but I could not see her.'

He described how he and another two men had managed to cling on to what was left of the dinghy. They floated for hours and the tide eventually led them close to the shore of the nearest Greek island.

'Some charity workers from the UK saw us,' he said. 'They helped us come ashore. We were weak as we had swallowed lots of water, and hypothermic as it was so cold.'

The workers had taken them to a refugee camp where they had looked after them for weeks. Months later the charity had organised for him to fly to the UK to start a new life. He was given a place at a hostel and he had eventually applied for asylum and was granted refugee status after six months.

'It was very hard,' sighed Muhammad. 'I needed to find job and a house but the charity help me so much.'

'Are you happy here?' Penny asked him.

'I know no one in UK,' he said. 'I have been very lonely, but it is safer than Iraq. Every day I think of my family, of Halima and our father and wonder where they are . . .'

His voice trailed off and his eyes filled with tears.

'I think Halima is dead,' he sighed. 'I think she has gone under the water and she is with Mama now and I will never see her again.'

'And now you send me a letter.' He smiled, wiping his eyes. 'And I feel happy again.'

'You've both been through so much,' I told him. 'I know how much Halima has missed you.'

I told him her story about how she had got to this country. His eyes were wide as I recounted how she'd travelled across Europe.

'My little sister, she is very brave,' he sighed. 'She must have been very frightened.'

I nodded.

'Understandably, she's been very traumatised and has found it difficult to settle,' I replied. 'It's been hard for her at school not speaking the language at first and she has struggled to make friends.

'I know at night she cries for your family and your mother.'

'She misses Mama.' He nodded. 'They were very close.'

'Your sister has been through a very hard time recently,' Penny told him.

As she explained what had happened with Abu Rasheed, Muhammad looked shocked.

'Syria?' he gasped. 'No, no, Halima would never go there.'

'We believe that she had been radicalised online and was planning to,' I told him.

He looked completely confused by the whole thing.

'When can I see her?' he asked. 'When can I see my sister?'

'We'll talk to Halima about it and if she's happy, then we'll set something up as soon as we can,' Penny told him.

Muhammad said he could get the train and come to my house.

I thought that would be a good idea as it meant Halima was somewhere comfortable where she felt safe. We couldn't automatically assume that their reunion would go well and I had to protect her interests in all of this.

'If and when you do meet Halima, please don't mention the things we told you about IS and Syria, unless she brings it up,' Penny told him. 'It's been an extremely difficult time for her and she's been doing so well lately. It's taken a lot for her to move on from this.'

'I understand,' he said.

'I pray that I can see her soon,' he told us as we left.

'We hope so too.' I smiled.

As I got into the car, my heart felt full.

'What a lovely young man,' I said.

I felt so excited for Halima and I knew this was going to mean so much to her.

'I can come back to your house now, Maggie, and talk to Halima after school if you want?' Penny suggested.

'Penny, would you have any objection if I told her about Muhammad instead?' I asked.

For once, there was some happy news, and I really wanted to be the one to pass it on.

'Of course.' She smiled.

Natalie was going to her nan's tonight after school so I picked Halima up and we headed home.

'Can I have a quick chat to you in the kitchen?' I asked her when we got in. She looked warily at me with her eyebrows raised, as if to say 'what now', but I couldn't wait a minute longer.

'Halima, I've got something really exciting to tell you.' I grinned. 'I'm so happy to say that we've found your brother. Penny and I went to see him today.'

Halima stared at me blankly.

'Do you understand what I'm telling you, flower?' I said gently. 'We've found Muhammad and he's in the UK. He lives in a city two hours away from here.'

Halima looked at me in total disbelief.

'My brother Muhammad?' she questioned.

I nodded.

'B-but I thought Muhammad was dead,' she gasped. 'Is it really him?'

I nodded.

'Are you sure?'

'Completely sure.' I smiled. 'I thought you were going to ask me that, so I made sure that I took some photos of him.'

I got my phone out of my bag and Halima practically wrenched it out of my hands. As soon as she saw the picture, she burst into tears.

'It is him!' she sobbed. 'He looks so pale and tall. Has he always been that tall? But it is him, Maggie,' she told me. 'It is really him.'

'I know.' I smiled, putting my arm around her. 'It's such brilliant news.'

For once she was crying happy tears.

'I told myself he was dead,' she wept. 'I believed he had gone under the water that night and drowned.'

'He thought that the same thing had happened to you,' I said. 'He was very tearful when we told him you were alive and well.'

Halima shook her head and stared at the photograph.

'When can I see him?' she asked. 'Does he have a phone? Can I ring him? Can I speak to him now, Maggie?'

'He does have a phone and I don't see why not,' I laughed.

When we had been to see him, Penny had asked if it was OK for us to give Halima his number.

Her hands were shaking as she rang the number.

'Muhammad,' she wept when he answered. 'Dear brother.'

She could hardly get her words out for crying. They chatted away in Arabic for around ten minutes.

'Yes, I will see you soon,' she told him.

At the end, I took the phone back and Halima cried again.

'I am so happy to hear his voice,' she wept. 'He sounded the same.'

I sent Penny a quick text to let her know they had spoken. She said she was going to ring him and set up a meeting. She texted me back ten minutes later.

Muhammad can't come tomorrow as he's at work, but we've arranged for him to come to your house on Thursday as he has the day off. Happy for Halima to have the day off school.

Halima was ecstatic when I told her the news.

'I wish it was Thursday now,' she sighed. 'I cannot wait that long.'

I ordered us a takeaway to celebrate and as the evening went on, she had so many questions.

'But how did he get here? When did he get here?'

I told her everything I knew. How he'd clung on to what

was left of the deflated dinghy for hours and was eventually rescued by the charity that had brought him to England. They'd helped him to seek asylum and eventually he'd found a job.

'So, he's been here longer than me?' she said, her eyes wide. 'All of this time and he's been so near.'

When Natalie came home, Halima ran to the front door to see her.

'Nat, Nat, I've found my brother,' she gasped. 'He's alive and he lives in England and he's coming to see me on Thursday.'

Nat looked shocked.

'Wow,' she gasped. 'That's so cool.'

'I thought he had drowned, Nat, but he is alive.' She smiled.

'I bet you're really happy,' she told her.

But I could tell by Natalie's face there was something bothering her. While Halima couldn't stop smiling, Natalie looked utterly miserable.

She hardly said a word and she took herself straight off to bed.

I went up to see her.

'Are you OK, lovey?' I asked her. 'You seem a bit down.'

'Nan wasn't good today,' she sighed. 'She was very poorly and the carer thinks she might have a chest infection. The doctor's coming out to see her later.'

'Oh, Nat, I'm sorry to hear that,' I told her.

I felt terrible, as in all of the excitement about Halima, I'd forgotten to ask Nat how her nan was. I knew with her disease, an infection like that could potentially kill her.

'I've got the carer's number so shall I ring her later and check how she is?'

Natalie nodded.

I had two girls both going through very different things. The happiness shone out of Halima's face but Natalie was worried and I knew she wouldn't sleep until I'd had an update from the carer.

I got through to her at last at around 10 p.m. After we got off the phone, I went up to Natalie, who was still wide awake.

'A nurse and a doctor went to see your nan,' I told her. 'They're giving her antibiotics via a drip and they're going to keep an eye on her. They said she's comfortable and she's sleeping.'

Natalie nodded.

'If it doesn't work, will she have to go to hospital?' she asked.

'Probably.' I nodded. 'But let's cross that bridge when we come to it.'

I gave her a hug and hoped she would sleep.

When I peered around Halima's door, I saw that she was wide awake too.

'You need to get some sleep, lovey, you have school in the morning,' I told her gently.

'What will we do when Muhammad comes round?' she asked me.

'You two can spend some time together and I'll make us some lunch,' I said. 'You're going to have a lot of catching up to do.'

She nodded and grinned.

That night when I went to bed, I couldn't sleep either. I was so happy for Halima but I still had a niggle of anxiety about her reunion with Muhammad. Even in situations where everyone seemed happy, you never truly knew if someone was going to turn up until the day, let alone predict how they were going to get along. I had been at too many family reunions over the years that hadn't gone the way everyone had expected, so I always preferred to err on the side of caution. I was also worried about Natalie. Peggy had been deteriorating for some time now and I knew it was a lot for Natalie to cope with. I was trying to do the best I could for both girls but sometimes being a foster parent felt like a constant juggle.

For the next two nights Halima hardly slept.

'I can't stop thinking about Muhammad and what I am going to say to him,' she said.

I was worried she was going to burn herself out by the time he arrived.

On the morning of his visit, she was practically bouncing off the walls with nervous excitement. Penny had rung him the night before and he'd confirmed that he was definitely coming.

'How will he know where to go?' Halima asked. 'What if he can't find the house?'

'Penny's sorted him out a train ticket and she's going to collect him from the train station and bring him here,' I told her, praying once again that everything went to plan.

'I know, I'll make kleicha,' she said. 'Muhammad loves them.'

I was grateful that making the cookies would give her a welcome distraction. I felt a little more at ease when Penny texted to say that she had picked Muhammad up.

'They're on their way,' I told Halima.

She ran upstairs to get changed and came down in a long black skirt and her favourite jumper. Then she sat by the window, waiting and watching for Penny's car to pull up outside.

I felt nervous too. I desperately wanted this to go well for her. *There's no reason why it shouldn't*, I told myself.

I was in the kitchen tidying up when I heard a loud shriek.

'He is here!' yelled Halima, running to the front door.

She opened it and flew down the path in her bare feet towards Muhammad and threw herself into his arms. They were both crying.

'As-salamu alaikum,' Muhammad said, burying his head in Halima's hair.

'I didn't think I would ever see you again,' sobbed Halima.

I smiled at Penny and I could see she was as choked up as I was.

'Come on, you two,' she said to them gently. 'I know you've got a lot of catching up to do so let's go inside.'

I need not have worried. Halima and Muhammad were so happy to see each other. She wouldn't leave him alone for a minute. She sat next to him on the sofa and wouldn't let go of his arm.

Penny and I left them to it and went into the kitchen to make us all a cup of tea.

'She's delighted to see him.' I smiled. 'It's so lovely to see.'

When we went back into the living room, they were still talking in Arabic to each other.

'We should try and speak in English,' she told him and he nodded.

'I try but my English is not as good as yours,' he told her.

As we drank our tea, Halima suddenly jumped up.

'I made you something,' she said, running off to the kitchen. She came back clutching a plate.

'Kleicha,' said Muhammad. 'Just like Mama's.'

'Not as good as Mama's but I tried my best,' replied Halima.

They also talked about their father. Muhammad had contacted friends who were still in Iraq and they were not able to tell him if their dad was still in prison.

'Poor Papa,' sighed Halima.

'Don't worry, we will find out what has happened to him and try to help him,' Muhammad reassured her.

Shortly afterwards, it was time for Penny to head back to the office.

'I can give Muhammad a lift back to the station later,' I told her.

The morning flew by. I left the siblings chatting while I did some cleaning and called Peggy's carer for an update to give Natalie. To my relief, the antibiotics seemed to be working for now and Peggy had improved slightly.

After lunch it was time to take Muhammad to the station. Halima suddenly got very tearful.

'I don't want you to go,' she told him, clinging on to him.

'I've got work tomorrow,' he told her. 'It's a new job so I cannot let them down.'

'Maggie, can he come to visit me again? Or can I go and see where he lives?' I asked.

'Let's talk to Penny,' I told her. 'You've got Muhammad's number so you can call him now whenever you want.'

I watched as they hugged goodbye.

Halima seemed a bit downcast for the rest of the day.

'I miss him,' she told me.

That evening I went to say goodnight and Halima was lying in bed staring at the ceiling. She was cuddling the cushion that she'd made with the photograph of her family on it.

'Maggie, can I ask you a question?' she said.

Before she had even opened her mouth, I already guessed what it was going to be.

'Can I go and live with Muhammad?' she said. 'I know he's an adult so he cannot live here with us. But he said he has a flat with two bedrooms. Could I sleep in the other one?'

'I'm afraid I can't make those decisions, lovey,' I told her. 'You would need to talk to Penny about it. And Muhammad would need to want that too. Everyone needs to be in agreement that it's the best thing for you. It's very early days and it's not something that can happen instantly.'

She nodded.

I didn't want to give her false hope. I could see that her brother clearly loved her, but he might not want the responsibility of his sixteen-year-old sister going to live with him permanently.

I could see the hope in Halima's eyes and I just prayed that she wasn't left heartbroken.

EIGHTEEN

Hope

I'd got my speech all prepared for Penny when I popped into Social Services to see her.

Even at breakfast this morning, Halima had been begging me to talk to Penny about Muhammad.

'Tell her he is my family and she has to let me live with my family,' she pleaded.

'I can't make any promises, flower, but I'll see what I can do,' I replied.

My worst fear was that Muhammad didn't want the same thing. Even though they had a good relationship, it was a big responsibility to become the legal guardian of a sixteen-year-old and he was entirely within his rights to say no.

'How did the rest of Muhammad's visit go yesterday after I'd left?' asked Penny as she made us both a cup of tea.

'It couldn't have gone better.' I smiled. 'It was lovely to see Halima so happy. She's felt so lost without her family and watching them together, I could just see how close they are.'

Then it came to the crunch. I explained that since Muhammad had left, Halima had constantly been asking if she could go and live with him permanently.

'I didn't want to get her hopes up until you'd spoken to Muhammad and I haven't made any promises,' I told Penny. 'But I can see how much she really wants this and I wondered if this is something Social Services could look at long term?'

Penny smiled knowingly.

'What is it?' I asked her.

'Funnily enough, Maggie, Muhammad rang me this morning and asked me exactly the same thing. He wants Halima to move in with him. In fact, he automatically assumed that she would be joining him.'

It was such a relief, I almost burst into tears. After everything Halima had been through, I was so worried about having to let her down.

'Kinship Care is definitely something we can look into,' Penny told me. 'And at this stage, I don't see any reason why it can't happen.'

Kinship Care was where children in the care system were looked after by someone they already knew, which could either be a relative or a friend. As Halima was sixteen, the rules were slightly more relaxed, but Muhammad would be subject to the usual Social Services checks. They would want to check that he didn't have a criminal record or had been in trouble with the police and that he was legally entitled to stay in the UK.

'He would also be entitled to some funding,' she added.

Social Services gave a regular allowance to the carer of the 'looked after' child to help with the costs of raising them.

As Muhammad was probably on a minimum wage, it was something that he would definitely need.

The second Halima got into the car after school with Natalie, she asked me about it.

'Did you speak to Penny? What did she say?'

'I did.' I smiled. 'The good news is Muhammad had already talked to Penny, saying that he wants you to go and live with him.'

She looked so happy.

'What?' gasped Natalie. 'You're leaving?'

'Yes,' said Halima. 'I'm going to go and live with my brother.'

'Aw,' sighed Natalie.

'Don't worry, she's not going just yet, Nat,' I told her gently.

When we got home, I had a quiet word with Halima.

'You know if you do go and live with Muhammad it will mean you starting at another new school?' I asked her.

It was a shame, as she had just began to make friends and seemed a lot more settled.

'I know but I do not mind,' she told me. 'My English is better now and I will have my brother to support me.'

As a child in the care system, she could choose which school she wanted to go to, and I offered to go and look at them with her and Muhammad.

'When can I go and live at the flat?' she asked excitedly. 'Can it be this weekend?'

'I'm afraid it's not as simple as that,' I told her.

I explained that Social Services had a responsibility to make sure that she was safe, and that Muhammad could cope with both working and looking after her.

'It's not going to happen overnight,' I told her. 'It might take up to six weeks to get everything sorted.'

Until then, she could still see Mohammad at weekends and after school on his day off.

'You can call each other whenever you want and spend more time with each other to get you both used to the idea.'

We arranged for Muhammad to come over for the day at the weekend and then Penny was going to take Halima to his flat the following Friday after school and she was going to spend the night there. On Saturday I went to pick her up from the train station.

'So how was it?' I asked.

'Good.' She smiled. 'I really liked the flat. Muhammad has a big TV and he'd just been paid so we had a kebab for tea.'

She said there was no furniture in the second bedroom, so she'd slept on an airbed that Mohammad had borrowed from a friend at work.

'Don't worry, if you move there permanently you won't have to sleep on the floor,' I told her.

Social Services would provide an allowance so she could buy a bed and some furniture.

Halima spoke to Muhammad every day and she saw him every weekend. In the meantime, she was still having her sessions at Unite with Sonia. I'd kept her updated about Halima's plans to move in with her brother. There was one issue that we had to address.

'Do you think she's still at risk of going to Syria?' I asked her.

I knew it was something Penny was going to be asking and Social Services had to be sure before letting her move.

'I honestly don't think she is,' replied Sonia. 'I think what happened was a huge shock for her. They got in touch with her when she was at her lowest. She'd just come to a new country, she felt alienated and was grief-stricken. But she's more settled now and the main thing is that she has her brother. I think with Muhammad around she feels a sense of family so she's not so alone.'

Sonia said Halima had recently offered to help her give talks to other young people.

'She wanted to tell them about her experiences to warn them about the dangers of radicalisation.'

'That's amazing.' I smiled.

'I think it's too soon for her to do that now, but I've said that perhaps she can come back in a few months,' replied Sonia.

I was so proud of Halima.

The Counter Terrorism Unit had also been looking into what happened and they had uncovered some background information about Abu Rasheed, which they had passed on to Penny. He was Algerian, in his late twenties and already had three wives and multiple children. One of his wives had died in a drone strike and two were now living in a camp in northern Syria as they had tried to escape.

'I feel like we have a responsibility to share this information with Halima,' Penny told me. 'Do you think she will be upset that he had other wives?'

I shook my head.

'I don't think for Halima it was ever about romantic love,' I sighed. 'For her I think it was more about having a sense of belonging and family of her own and somewhere to call home.

'She was never particularly romantic in her messages to him. I think she was more in love with the idea than the actual person.'

I sat with Halima while Penny told her what the police had found out.

'I do not care,' she said, unflinching. 'I never want to think about him and Zahra again. I was lonely and sad then, but I am not now. I know they're not good people or good Muslims.'

Penny handed her a printout of the information in case she wanted to read it in her own time. But Halima took the papers and tore them into pieces and threw them in the bin before walking out of the kitchen.

'I think that's her way of saying that she's moved on,' I told Penny.

'I hope so,' she said.

There was no way of knowing for sure, but I did truly believe that Halima had moved on. Penny and Sonia had also talked to Muhammad about it and he knew the signs to look out for and to talk to Halima about it.

The weeks passed and all the checks on Muhammad came back clear.

'The good news is we can start organising your move over to your brother's house,' Penny told Halima.

I knew both her and Muhammad were impatient to get things moving and we had secured her a place at a new school that she liked. It was very multicultural and the head teacher had proudly told us how more than fifty languages were spoken by the pupils and staff. They also had another four pupils at the school who had come from Iraq.

Halima had arrived in this country with nothing, so she still didn't have a huge amount of stuff. We arranged to drive her and most of her things over to the flat one Saturday morning and then she would come back for one last night with us before leaving for good the next day.

Natalie wanted to come too, and I knew it would be nice for her to see where Halima was moving to. We packed up her things in cardboard boxes and dropped them off at the flat.

Social Services had paid for a bed, a wardrobe and a chest of drawers but her room still looked very bare and basic.

'Right,' I said to Halima and Natalie. 'We're off to IKEA.'

As a leaving present, I wanted to buy her a few things to make her room look more homely. Natalie pushed the trolley while Halima chose a rug that she liked and some cushions, as well as some bedding, curtains and a lamp. Then we went back to the flat to transform it. It took us a good few hours to get everything out, make the bed and put the curtains up.

'It looks so much better,' I said, putting the cushion with the photo of her family on it onto her bed.

As a surprise, I'd also got frames for the sketches she'd done of Iraq so we could put them on the wall.

'It looks amazing,' said Halima. 'It's like a different room.'

We'd also picked up a few plants and cushions for the living room and another rug to make it more cosy.

'Thank you, Maggie,' said Halima, giving me a hug.

'Muhammad will think he's got the wrong flat when he comes back from work tonight,' I joked.

Then we drove back to my house for Halima's last night with us.

The following day, I'd invited a few people round for a little goodbye party for Halima. Emaa and Paul came with their children Hattie and William, Halima's friend Poppy came and Miss Morgan, the art teacher from Halima's school. Penny, Becky and Sonia popped in as well as Louisa and Charlie. Muhammad came along too as Halima was keen for everyone to meet him. I made a buffet and everyone chatted and helped themselves.

I was so pleased that Louisa and Charlie had made it.

'How are you doing, lovey?' I asked Louisa as I caught her in a quiet corner. I was constantly worrying about her and today she looked pale and gaunt.

'Are you OK?' I sighed. 'You don't look well.'

'No, no, I'm fine,' she said.

But she wouldn't look me in the eye, and I could tell that something was bothering her.

'What is it, flower?' I asked her. 'You can tell me.'

Her eyes were wet with tears.

'I didn't want to tell you just yet as we haven't had the scan yet, but I'm pregnant again, Maggie,' she told me. 'I'm feeling as sick as a dog, just like I did last time.'

'Oh, lovey, that's wonderful news.' I smiled. 'I'm so happy for you.'

'I know it should be but I'm so scared,' she told me, her eyes wide. 'What if the same thing happens again? I don't think I can go through losing another baby after Dominic. My heart won't take it.'

'I know I can't make any promises, but the hospital will monitor you closely. Remember what the doctor told you – there's no medical reason why it should happen again,' I reassured her.

I desperately wanted to put my arms around her and tell her that everything was going to be OK but I couldn't. Her naivety about the world had been destroyed when Dominic had died, and I knew she wouldn't truly believe it until she was holding a healthy baby in her arms.

'I'll be here for you every step of the way,' I reassured her.

'Thank you, Maggie.' She smiled.

I was so happy about Louisa's news and it was a lovely, joyous afternoon. But despite all the fun of the day, I knew that it was going to end with a goodbye. I could see Halima was getting emotional as people gradually left.

Before Miss Morgan left, I noticed her hand Halima a large square parcel wrapped in tissue paper and they both walked over to me.

'Maggie, I have made you a goodbye present,' Halima said shyly.

'Halima did this at our art club and I helped her to frame it,' added Ms Morgan.

I unwrapped it to reveal the most incredible painting. It was of the back of a woman's head. She was sitting down at a table looking through some patio doors out at a garden. It was a sunny day, the sky was a vivid blue and the garden was filled with flowers.

'Gosh it's beautiful,' I sighed. 'I love the colours. Is it me?' I asked her.

'Yes, Maggie.' Halima smiled. 'You are sitting at the kitchen table looking out at your garden.'

'Our theme at art club that week was hope,' said Ms Morgan.

'And I wanted to paint you, Maggie, because you gave me hope,' Halima said. 'Thank you.'

I was lost for words, but my eyes filled with tears.

'I honestly don't know what to say,' I said, the words choking in my throat. 'I'm so pleased that I could do that for you, Halima.'

She'd lost her entire family and had been on the most traumatic journey imaginable. To know that I could offer her a home and give her hope was the biggest compliment that she could ever have paid me.

'I'll treasure this always,' I told her. 'I feel so privileged to have helped you.'

Then, when everyone else had gone, it was time to say our goodbyes. As always, I wanted to try and keep things upbeat and positive for Natalie and Halima's sake. Neither of them needed to see me weeping and wailing.

Natalie gave Halima a goodbye hug.

'I'm going to miss you so much,' she told her.

Then it was my turn.

I gave Halima a huge hug.

'I feel so sad to say goodbye to you,' she sighed.

'It's not really goodbye,' I told her. 'You'll only be a train ride away so you can come back and visit whenever you want.'

'And we'll come and see you,' added Natalie, who I knew was going to miss her very much.

But I knew it wasn't ever the same as having someone in your home.

'Go and be happy with your brother,' I whispered to her. 'You deserve it.'

Halima nodded and I could see that she was doing her best not to cry. We hugged Muhammad too and then Natalie and I stood at the window and waved them off. We watched as they laughed and chatted with each other as they walked down the road towards the station. A family reunited at last.

A note from Maggie

At the time Halima came to live with me, Islamic State, or IS, and so-called jihadi brides were a relatively new phenomenon. Now radicalisation is something that sadly is becoming increasingly common, particularly online and via social media, which provide terrorists with an easy way to connect with people.

It's been reported that around one hundred British women and girls have left the UK to join IS. That's 12 per cent of all British citizens who have travelled to Syria and Iraq to join the group. At least sixty British children are said to be currently trapped in north-east Syria after fleeing areas held by IS during the recent escalation in fighting. Figures compiled by a UK-based charity suggest many of the children are under five years old and all were born to British parents suspected of joining IS.

When I see heartbreaking statistics like this or read stories in newspapers, I'm just so thankful we discovered what was happening to Halima in time. The alternative doesn't bear thinking about. Halima was one of the lucky ones. She and Muhammad made a new life for themselves in the UK and we kept in touch. I know it was a struggle for them at times, especially for Muhammad as there were periods when he was out of work. However, they had each other and Halima eventually left school and went to art college. Several years later, they have yet to return to Iraq and sadly they're still searching to find out what happened to their father.

Acknowledgements

Thank you to my children, Tess, Pete and Sam, who are such a big part of my fostering today; however, I had not met you when Halima came into my home. To my wide circle of fostering friends – you know who you are! Your support and your laughter are valued. To my friend Andrew B for your continued encouragement and care. Thanks also to Heather Bishop who spent many hours listening and enabled this story to be told, my literary agent Rowan Lawton and to Anna Valentine and Marleigh Price at Seven Dials for giving me the opportunity to share these stories.

DADDY'S LITTLE SOLDIER

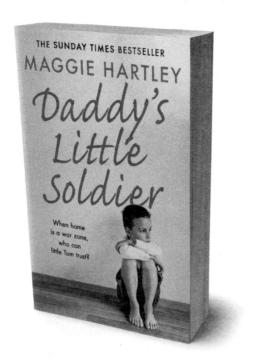

Tom has been taken into care following concerns that his dad is struggling to cope after the death of Tom's mum. When Maggie meets Tom's dad Mark, a stern ex-soldier and strict disciplinarian, it's clear that Tom's life at home without his mummy has been a constant battlefield. Can Maggie help Mark to raise a son and not a soldier? Or is little Tom going to lose his daddy too?

PLEASE, DON'T TAKE MY SISTERS

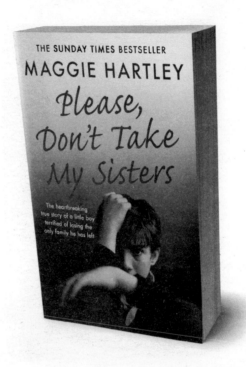

Leo's little sisters are the only family he has left in the world. But when Social Services begin to look at rehoming the little girls without their troubled older brother, the siblings' whole world comes crashing down. Can Maggie fight to keep the children together? Or will Leo lose the only love he's ever known?

A DESPERATE CRY FOR HELP

Meg arrives at Maggie's after a fire destroys the children's home she's been living in. But traumatised by the fire, and angry and vulnerable, having been put into care by her mother, Meg is lashing out at everyone around her. Can Maggie reach this damaged little girl before it's too late? And before Meg's destructive behaviour puts Maggie's life — and the lives of the other children in her care — at risk?

TINY PRISONERS

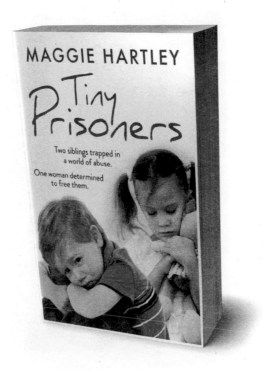

Evie and Elliot are scrawny, filthy and wide-eyed with fear when they turn up on foster carer Maggie Hartley's doorstep. They're too afraid to leave the house and any intrusion of the outside world sends them into a panic. It's up to Maggie to unlock the truth of their heartbreaking upbringing, and to help them learn to smile again.

THE LITTLE GHOST GIRL

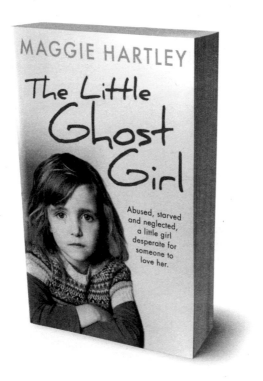

Ruth is a ghost of a girl when she arrives into foster carer Maggie Hartley's care. Pale, frail and withdrawn, it's clear to Maggie that Ruth had seen and experienced things that no 11-year-old should have to. Ruth is in desperate need of help, but can Maggie get through to her and unearth the harrowing secret she carries?

TOO YOUNG TO BE A MUM

When sixteen-year-old Jess arrives on foster carer Maggie Hartley's doorstep with her newborn son Jimmy, she has nowhere else to go. With Social Services threatening to take baby Jimmy into care, Jess knows that Maggie is her only chance of keeping her son. Can Maggie help Jess learn to become a mum?

WHO WILL LOVE ME NOW?

At just ten years old, Kirsty has already suffered a lifetime of heartache and suffering. When her latest foster carers decide they can no longer cope, Kirsty comes to live with Maggie. Reeling from this latest rejection, the young girl is violent and hostile, and Social Services fear that she may be a danger to those around her. Maggie finds herself in an impossible position, one that calls into question her decision to become a foster carer in the first place...

BATTERED, BROKEN, HEALED

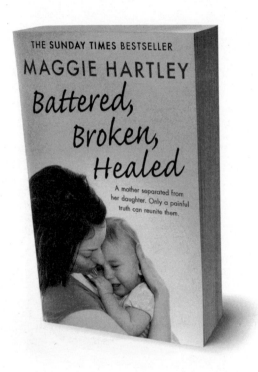

THE SUNDAY TIMES BESTSELLER

MAGGIE HARTLEY

Battered,
Broken,
Healed

A mother separated from
her daughter. Only a painful
truth can reunite them.

Six-week-old baby Jasmine comes to stay with Maggie after she is removed from her home. Neighbours have repeatedly called the police on suspicion of domestic violence, but her timid mother Hailey vehemently denies that anything is wrong. Can Maggie persuade Hailey to admit what's going on behind closed doors so that mother and baby can be reunited?

SOLD TO BE A WIFE

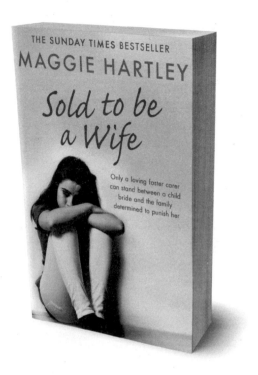

Fourteen-year-old Shazia has been taken into care over fears that her family are planning to send her to Pakistan for an arranged marriage. But with Shazia denying everything and with Social Services unable to find any evidence, Shazia is eventually allowed to return home. But when Maggie wakes up a few weeks later in the middle of the night to a call from the terrified Shazia, it looks like her worst fears have been confirmed...

DENIED A MUMMY

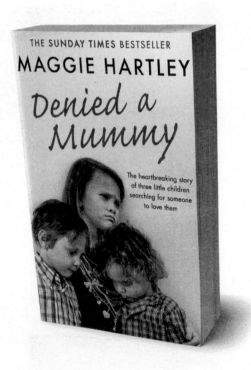

Maggie has her work cut out for her when her latest placement arrives on her doorstep; two little boys, aged five and seven, and their eight-year-old sister. Having suffered extensive abuse and neglect, Maggie must slowly work through their trauma with love and care. But when a couple is approved to adopt the siblings, alarm bells start to ring. Maggie tries to put her own fears to one side but she can't shake the feeling of dread as she waves goodbye to them. Will these vulnerable children ever find a forever family?

TOO SCARED TO CRY

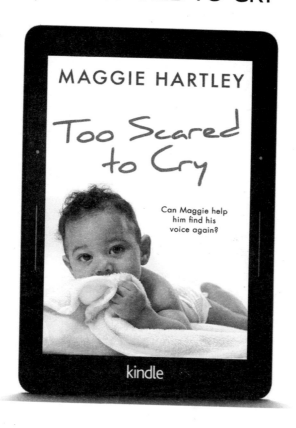

A baby too scared to cry. Two toddlers too scared to speak. This is the dramatic short story of three traumatised siblings, whose lives are transformed by the love of foster carer Maggie Hartley.

A FAMILY FOR CHRISTMAS

A tragic accident leaves the life of toddler Edward changed forever and his family wracked with guilt. Will Maggie be able to help this family grieve for the son they've lost and learn to love the little boy he is now? And will Edward have a family to go home to at Christmas?

THE GIRL NO ONE WANTED

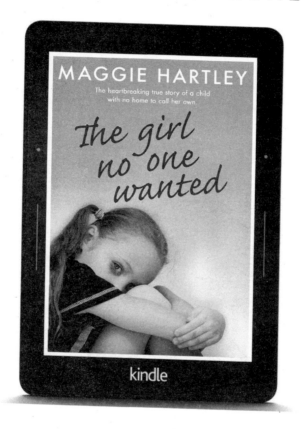

Eleven-year-old Leanne is out of control. With over forty placements in her short life, no local foster carers are willing to take in this angry and damaged little girl. Maggie is Leanne's only hope, and her last chance. If this placement fails, Leanne will have to be put in a secure unit. Where most others would simply walk away, Maggie refuses to give up on the little girl who's never known love.

IS IT MY FAULT, MUMMY?

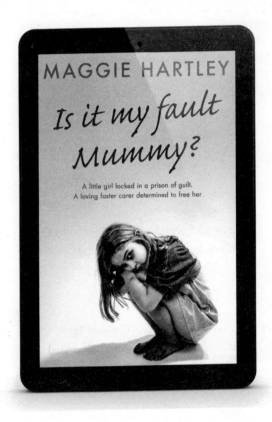

Seven-year-old Paris is trapped in a prison of guilt. Devastated after the death of her baby brother, Joel, Maggie faces one of the most heartbreaking cases yet as she tries to break down the wall of guilt surrounding this damaged little girl.

Credits

Maggie Hartley and Seven Dials would like to thank everyone at Orion who worked on the publication of *Groomed to be a Bride*.

Editorial
Marleigh Price

Copy editor
Clare Wallis

Proof reader
Jane Howard

Audio
Paul Stark
Amber Bates

Contracts
Anne Goddard
Paul Bulos
Jake Alderson

Design
Rachael Lancaster
Joanna Ridley
Nick May

Editorial Management
Jane Hughes
Alice Davis

Finance
Jasdip Nandra
Afeera Ahmed
Elizabeth Beaumont
Sue Baker

Marketing
Brittany Sankey

Production
Katie Horrocks

Publicity
Kate Moreton

Sales
Laura Fletcher
Esther Waters
Victoria Laws
Rachael Hum
Ellie Kyrke-Smith
Frances Doyle
Georgina Cutler

Operations
Jo Jacobs
Sharon Willis
Lisa Pryde
Lucy Brem